FIGHTING TECHNIQUES OF A
US MARINE

1941-1945

TRAINING, TECHNIQUES, AND WEAPONS

Leo J. Daugherty III

MBI Publishing Company

This edition first published in 2000 by
MBI Publishing Company
729 Prospect Avenue
PO Box 1, Osceola
WI 54020-0001 USA

MBI Publishing Company books are also available at discounts in bulk quantity
for industrial or sales-promotional use. For details write to Special Sales Manager
at Motorbooks International Wholesalers & Distributors, 729 Prospect Avenue,
PO Box 1, Osceola, WI 54020-0001 USA.

Library of Congress Cataloging-in-Publication Data available.

ISBN: 0-7603-0930-2

Editorial and design by
Amber Books Ltd
Bradley's Close
74-77 White Lion Street
London
N1 9PF

Project Editor: Charles Catton
Editor: David Norman
Design: Jeremy Williams
Picture Research: TRH Pictures Ltd

Printed in Italy - Nuova GEP, Cremona

Picture credits
Leo J. Daugherty: 30 (US Dept. of Defense), 33 (US Dept. of Defense), 42 (US Dept. of Defense), 50 (US Dept. of Defense), 51 (US Dept. of Defense), 53 (US Dept. of Defense), 54 (US Dept. of Defense), 57, 60 (US Marine Corps), 78 (b) (US Dept. of Defense), 83, 85 (US Dept. of Defense). **TRH Pictures**: 6 (US National Archives), 8 (US Navy), 10 (US Navy), 11 (US Marine Corps), 12 (US National Archives), 13 (US Marine Corps), 15 (US Marine Corps), 16 (US Marine Corps), 17 US Marine Corps), 18 (US Marine Corps), 19 (US Marine Corps), 22, 23 (IWM), 24 (US Marine Corps), 25, 27 (US Dept. of Defense), 28 (US Navy), 32 (US Marine Corps), 34 (US Marine Corps), 35, 37 (US Marine Corps), 38, 39 (US Dept. of Defense), 40, 43 (US Marine Corps), 44, 45, 47, 48 (US Marine Corps), 55, 56, 61 (US National Archives), 62, 63, 64, 67, 68 (US Marine Corps), 69, 71, 72, 73 (US Dept. of Defense), 75 (US National Archives), 76, 78-79, 80, 84 (US Marine Corps), 86, 88, 90 (US Marine Corps), 91, 92.

Artwork credits
Aerospace Publishing: 26 (b). **De Agostini UK**: 9, 21, 31, 41, 46, 77, 93. **Amber Books**: 87. **Bob Garwood**: 26 (t). **Patrick Mulrey**: 14, 70 (l), 74. **Gerald Wood**: 36 (both), 52 (both), 58, 66, 70 (r), 82.

CONTENTS

CHAPTER 1

The US Marine Corps: 1919–1945 Organization and Roles

> The US Marine Corps entered the twentieth century looking for a new role. Blooded in World War I and the minor wars of the 1920s and 1930s, the Marine Corps spent much of the interwar period training and perfecting the methods that would stand it in good stead for the Pacific campaigns of World War II.

FOR THE UNITED STATES MARINE CORPS, its performance during World War II was a vindication of its tactical and operational expertise gained during World War I (1917–1918). Furthermore, the development of the advanced base concept, formulated in the period (1908–1914) prior to the Marine Corps' involvement in World War I, and which Marine officials later 'grafted' onto its experiences in the trenches in France, greatly contributed to the formulation of amphibious warfare tactics and led to the defeat of not only Imperial Japan but also Nazi Germany. Indeed, both the American and British armies were able to launch a series of heavy blows against the island outposts of both Germany and Japan thanks largely to the pioneering efforts of Marine officers and enlisted men during the budget-starved interwar era of the 1920s and 1930s.

When the US Marine Corps landed on Guadalcanal on 7 August 1942, much of its organization, tactics, and fighting techniques had been well established during the interwar period (1919–40). Undoubtedly, the Corps' concepts of warfighting had been shaped by its participation in World War I as part of the Fourth Marine Brigade, attached to the US Army's 2nd Division ('The Indianhead') as a part of the American Expeditionary Forces. During the interwar period

up to May 1942, Marines still carried the venerable M1903 'Springfield' rifle, wore the Model 1910 Field Infantry Pack and cartridge belt (known by Marines as '782' gear), and up until the Battle of Midway wore the M1917A1 steel helmet used in World War I; used the same training manuals and infantry drill regulations as the American doughboys during World War I and the interwar period, and were organized along similar Army Tables of Organization up until the 1930s. What, then, distinguished Marines from their Army counterparts? The answer is simply, not much. The exceptions to this are the Corps' smaller tactical formations, recruit training, naval heritage, and its esprit d'corps. Since the Marines are a part of the Department of the US Navy, and receive their operating funds from the Navy, they have and always will be considered as an integral part of a fleet's landing component.

FROM ADVANCED BASE FORCE TO AMPHIBIOUS ASSAULT, 1898–1931

From the dawn of the new 'steel' Navy in the 1880s, the US Marine Corps had been a force looking for a role. The transition from sail to steam meant an end to the Corps' traditional mission as a naval security force and as secondary gun crews aboard the Navy's men-o'-war and, unknown to Marine leaders at the time, ushered in a new, and larger mission as a base seizure and defence force, capable of seizing advanced naval bases used by the Navy's ships as refuelling

Left: Two US Marines survey the landscape during the fighting on Saipan in mid-1944. The Marine in the foreground is armed with an M1 Garand rifle, while the other one kneeling is armed with the shorter M1 Carbine.

Above: A US Marine shipboard detachment in the late 1880s. As well as acting as a landing force or boarding party when needed, Marines manned the secondary guns aboard ship; roles that had changed little since Napoleonic times.

points strategically located to defend American lives, property, and interests in Asia and in the Caribbean Sea.

Marines were the first US force to take offensive action against Spanish forces in the Philippines, and a Marine unit, commanded by 1st Lieutenant Dion Williams, seized the Spanish naval base at Cavite there on 1 May 1898. Another Marine force, commanded by Lieutenant Colonel Robert W. Huntington, landed at Fisherman's Point, near Guantanamo Bay, Cuba on 10 June 1898, in order to establish a coaling station for the US Fleet then blockading the Cuban coastline to prevent Admiral Cervera's Spanish fleet from escaping into the Atlantic. Marines likewise participated in the seizure of Puerto Rico, and contributed land forces to the fighting on Cuban soil. In effect, the landings at Cavite and Guantanamo Bay signalled the origins of the advanced base force mission, the predecessor to the amphibious warfare mission.

From 1900 to 1914, Marines undertook several advanced base exercises in the Philippines and on the Puerto Rican island of Culebra, and established a school, first at New London, Connecticut (1910), and then later at the Philadelphia Navy Yard, for Marine officers and enlisted men to study

the theoretical and practical application of methods to establish an advanced naval base. Other Marine officers, a group that included Majors John H. Russell, Robert H. Dunlap, Eli K. Cole, Dion Williams, and Captain Earl H. 'Pete' Ellis – all of whom would play a critical role in the development of amphibious warfare doctrine in the interwar period – attended the Navy War College, located at Newport, Rhode Island, where they wrote and lectured on the advanced base force, and its role during a naval campaign.

Foremost among these officers were Lieutenant Colonel Eli K. Cole (later Major General), Majors (later Major General Commandant) John H. Russell, Dion Williams (later Brigadier General), as well as Captain (later Lieutenant Colonel) Earl H. 'Pete' Ellis, all of whom made significant contributions to the size and composition of the advanced base force prior to World War I. Both LtCol Cole and Major Russell believed that any advanced base defence force should consist of at least a regiment comprised of twelve companies of 150 men, each organized into three 600-men battalions, for a total regimental strength of 1800 officers and men. Major Williams suggested that any advanced base force should consist of two regiments each of 1200 men, with each regiment assigned to a specific role of being either 'fixed' – manning permanently emplaced guns and positions – or the 'mobile' regiment, able to reinforce or seize an advanced base as part of a fleet train.

The actual force that emerged approximated that of Major Williams' force of two regiments each of 1200 men, and remained the size of an advanced base force felt necessary to accomplish either base seizure or defence. From 1907 to 1914, Marines participated in several advanced base exercises, culminating with a large manoeuvre held on the Puerto Rican island of Culebra during the US Navy's fleet exercises in January 1914. Along with the 'fixed' and 'mobile' forces of the Advanced Base Force, the newly-formed Marine air component, headed by 1stLts Bernard L. Smith and William M. McIlvain, participated in the exercise as well, and made a small, though significant, contribution in demonstrating the value of air power to an advanced base force.

Despite these early, enthusiastic beginnings of the advanced base force concept, the outbreak of political chaos on the island of Hispaniola in Haiti, and its neighbour, the Dominican Republic, required the deployment of two Marine brigades, virtually stripping the US Marine Corps of manpower and funds to continue experimentation and refinement of the advanced base force concept. Furthermore, the outbreak of war in Europe in August 1914 diverted attention and eventually resources away from the continued efforts of the Marines to develop the advanced base force. Theoretically, however, the advanced base force remained an important mission of the Marines, as codified by the General Board of the Navy, an *ad hoc* committee that discussed and made policy recommendations to the Secretary of the Navy and the various US Navy bureaus.

The Marines enter World War I

When the United States entered World War I on the side of the Allies, the Marines contributed two brigades, the 4th and the 5th, to the American Expeditionary Forces headed by General John J. Pershing. The 4th Brigade, comprised of the 5th and 6th Marine Regiments and the 6th Machine Gun Battalion, and commanded at times by Marine and Army officers, eventually became part of the US 2nd Division, commanded by Major General John A. Lejeune, a Marine general, and later the thirteenth commandant of the Corps. Participation in World War I by the Marines proved to be extremely beneficial, as the Marine officers, most notably MajGen Lejeune and a host of company and field grade officers who would guide the Corps through the interwar period, witnessed the advent of modern technological warfare, and the possibilities that it held out for the Marine Corps' advanced base mission, in terms of weaponry, organization, staff work, tactics, and air power. The participation of the Marines in the fighting was substantial, despite the fact that no more than 26,755 Marines saw service in France at

A US Marine Corps captain stationed in Iceland in January 1942. His uniform is little changed from that used by the Marines in World War I, and this captain is wearing a French Croix de Guerre on his breast, which was awarded to the 5th and 6th Marines for their service in France in 1917-18. He wears the M1917 service helmet.

Above: US Marines stand in formation at Guantanamo Bay, Cuba in June 1898. Marines were the first ashore during the war with Spain in 1898. These Marines belonged to Lt Col Robert W. Huntington's Marine battalion.

any one time; this from a force that expanded from a pre-war level of 13,000 to 75,000 Marines at the war's conclusion. Yet the real contribution, in terms of the advanced base and later the amphibious assault mission, came in the training that it offered Marine officers and enlisted men, and the infrastructure that it created in terms of recruiting, basic and branch officer and enlisted individual training, and staff work. As the interwar era demonstrated, many of the lessons of World War I remained an important part of Marine training and tactical organization up to the eve of World War II.

Organization of the Marine Brigade, 1917–1918

The Marines adopted the US Army's tables of organization, which called for a regiment comprised of three battalions organized from a four-company infantry battalion, with companies consisting of 256 officers and men each, with an attached machine gun company, headquarters, and supply companies with an aggregate strength of 2759 officers and men, larger than either the British or French regiments, which by the spring of 1918 had been severely battered by the German Michael Offensive of 21 March 1918.

While some Marines served in France, others remained in the US, or were sent by Headquarters Marine Corps (HQMC) to the US–Mexican border to protect the Texan oil fields; or to Cuba to guard vital US interests, particularly the sugar cane fields, against saboteurs. For practical purposes, however, the advanced base force concept remained moribund. It would only be revitalized at the war's end, and even then on a limited basis, as demobilisation and manpower shortages, as well as a return to expeditionary duty in the West Indies, took its toll on the Corps' operating forces.

Despite the best efforts of MajGen George Barnett, the Major General Commandant of the Marine Corps, to revive the advanced base force concept, it was left to his successor, MajGen John A. Lejeune, a highly-decorated and proven combat leader, to guide the Marine Corps through the 1920s. From 1922 to 1925, the US Marine Corps engaged in several landing or 'advanced base' exercises off Culebra, Panama, and Oahu, Territory of Hawaii, that demonstrated just how far the Corps had to go in the development of an effective landing doctrine.

THE MARINE CORPS EXPEDITIONARY FORCE AND THE EXERCISES OF THE 1920S

In the postwar realignment of the Corps, MajGen Lejeune renamed the advanced base force the Marine Corps

Expeditionary Force (MCEF), a change that was more administrative than substantive, since the force retained its basic mission of 'seizing and defending' advanced naval bases, 'and to supply a mobile force to accompany the Fleet for operations on shore in support of a naval campaign'. As designed by HQMC, the MCEF 'should be of such size, organization, armament and equipment as may be required by the plan of naval operations . . . .' One mission added by MajGen Lejeune stressed the Marine Corps' use as a naval expeditionary force '. . . for the purpose of carrying out the foreign policy of our Government, or for emergency use at home'. The force was to be based at the Marine Barracks, Quantico, VA, under the command of the Commander-in-Chief US Fleet during wartime. Even with the redesignation and revitalization of the MCEF, manpower and budget cuts severely hampered HQMC's plans to find a role for the US Marine Corps in the ongoing planning for a potential war with Japan, referred to then as 'Orange'.

A plan, postulated by Major (later LtCol) Earl H. 'Pete' Ellis, author of the US Marine Corps' basic warfighting plan 'Advanced Base Operations in Micronesia, OPLAN 712-D' (1921), provided the US Marine Corps with just that type of mission. As Ellis saw it, in any war with Japan in the Pacific Ocean area, both the US Navy and Army would have to fight their way across thousands of miles of ocean comprised of several major island groups, most notably the Marianas,

Above: US Marines formed part of the international force stationed in Peking after the Boxer Rebellion. Here two Marines are photographed with members of the British, German, Japanese, Russian and French armed forces.

Marshalls, and Palau Islands. While the Army would be concerned with retaking the Philippines, it would be left to the Navy and Marine Corps to seize and defend a series of islands in order for the fleet to replenish itself as it fought the Japanese fleets across the vast stretches of the Pacific.

Part of the US Marine Corps' mission would be to 'retake' the islands handed to Japan as mandates by the League of Nations in any naval campaign. Ellis's plan assumed that these islands would in fact be fortified by Japan, in direct violation of the terms of the Washington Naval Treaty (1920–1), and their capture would fall to the Marines. Although Ellis died in the Palau Islands in mysterious circumstances, MajGen Lejeune accepted his warfighting plan as the basic guideline by which the US Marine Corps trained and organized its forces during the 1920s and 1930s. As World War II demonstrated, Ellis wasn't far off the mark, as Marines had to retake, at considerable expense of lives and material, each of the island groups mentioned above, as well as several others not studied by LtCol Ellis.

Even as Ellis wrote his warfighting plan, Marines continued to exercise and train as part of the MCEF. From January

Above: US Marines served in World War I in France as part of the 4th Marine Brigade. Here, a squad of leathernecks attack a fortified German position in the town of Vaux near Chateau-Thierry in June 1918.

to April 1922, a Marine expeditionary detachment under the command of LtCol Richard M. Cutts participated in exercises held at Guantanamo Bay and at Culebra. The main purpose of the first exercise, conducted by the 9th Company, 10th Marine Regiment and carried out at the US Naval Base, Guantanamo Bay, Cuba, sought to test specifically the landing of a 155mm (6.1in) howitzer and an accompanying 10.1-tonne (10-ton) tractor from ship to shore in small boats, where 'close attention was paid to the training of the gun's crews and special details, the hardening of the men, and testing out of all the material, and communication'.

Fleet Manoeuvres at Culebra

This same force, re-embarked aboard the USS *Florida*, then proceeded to the island of Culebra, and augmented by three officers and 100 men, participated in the annual fleet manoeuvres on that Caribbean island. Here, Marines successfully landed and demonstrated that 'artillery up to and

including 155mm guns and 10-ton tractors could be transported by a battleship and landed in ship's boats'. LtCol Cutts tempered his remarks, however, when in a further after action report he stated that the 'conditions must be favorable (i.e. a calm sea and moderate surf, as well as a suitable landing area) to land such a force'. He recommended that a lighter be constructed, modelled on the British 'Beetle' or armoured boat used during the failed landings at Gallipoli. In his annual report to the Secretary of the Navy for 1922, MajGen Lejeune commented that 'the exercises of 1922 were defensive in their nature, they brought out the difficulties of attack in landing operations against hostile opposition and the further presumption that the Marine Corps should be preparing for offensive landing operations in addition to the defensive advanced base work.'

From 1923 through February the MCEF participated in the annual fleet manoeuvres (FLEXES) under the command of BrigGen Eli K. Cole. Conducted at first in the Canal Zone and on Culebra, the 3330-man Marine force split between an 'offensive' or 'Black' force, and a 'defensive' or 'Blue' force (commanded by Col Dion Williams) stationed on Culebra. After the Marines 'seized' the locks in Panama, the 'Black' Force, commanded by BrigGen Cole, moved on to Culebra, where the 'Blue' force successfully repelled the attacking 'Black' force.

While it had been proven that Marines could 'repel' a landing, the exercise demonstrated that they had a long way to go in conducting a ship-to-shore landing on a hostile beachhead. The exercise once again brought to the fore the need for better landing craft for both men and material. They tested two different types of landing craft: an artillery lighter or 'beetle' boat (so called because of its armoured shell around the hull of the boat), and an amphibious 'tank' built and designed by inventor Walter Christie, which was launched by an off-shore submarine. Carrying a 75mm (2.95in) howitzer, the tank initially made its way to shore with little difficulty, but it soon floundered and was forced to return to the submarine from where it had been launched. Although the Christie amphibious tank later made it to shore (after the exercise had finished), it had been determined that it was unseaworthy, and that further work had to be done to bring more decisive results.

The last major exercise of the decade occurred in April 1925 when a 1500-man Marine force, simulating a Marine attacking force of 42,000 men, participated in the annual fleet exercises off Oahu, Territory of Hawaii. Commanded by Col Robert H. Dunlap, one of the Marine Corps' main advocates of landing operations, with the officers of the US Marine Corps' Field Officers Course (based at Quantico) acting as members of the 'Blue' Expeditionary Force staff, Marines demonstrated marked improvement during this exercise, though once again the after action report cited the need for 'a boat suitable for landing the first waves ashore on a defended coast', and that these boats be both provided in a size capable of being carried on transports and able to be mass-produced in the event of war. Thus, the main problem appeared to be the lack of a suitable landing boat capable of transporting Marines and their equipment ashore, a problem not overcome until the mid-1930s. In defence of the Marines, however, HQMC maintained an active search for just such a landing craft, with experiments that continued off and on into the end of the decade.

The deployment of a substantial force of Marines to China in 1923 (later *en masse* in 1927) as well as another force to Nicaragua beginning in December 1926 and January 1927, signalled an end not only to participation with the fleet in its annual exercises, but also the efforts of the Marine Corps Schools at the Marine Barracks, Quantico, VA, to initiate a change in its curriculum on land operations to include landing and expeditionary operations. This had to wait until 1930, when a board specially appointed by MajGen Commandant Ben H. Fuller recommended such changes in the Field Officer's and Company Officer's Courses, to place more emphasis on the role of the Marine Corps with the fleet, as opposed to direct service on land in conjunction with the Army. Yet along with the changes that Marines eventually implemented at the MCS came the tactical reorganization of the MCEF into the Fleet Marine Force, or FMF, which remained unchanged in basic form as that with which the Marines went to war in 1941.

Evolution of a New Role

This change in operational philosophy did not occur overnight. Instead, it was an evolutionary process that began after the 1925 Oahu Maneuvers. After the Washington Naval Conference and its non-fortification clauses regarding US island possessions, notably Guam and the Philippines, Marine and Army officers attending the Army War College in Washington, D.C., and the Naval War College at Newport, Rhode Island, began to examine the question of the composition, organization, and employment of an expeditionary force. Whereas Army officers believed that a force no smaller than a division and no larger than a corps of three divisions should be assigned such a role, Marine officers, due to the Corps' being 15,000 strong, believed such a force should number anywhere from 11,085 to 12,918, comprised of two infantry brigades, artillery, combat support, combat service support elements, and an attached air element of not less than a squadron of pursuit planes and light bombers.

Below: During an exercise in the Caribbean, Marines land a 75mm (2.95in) howitzer from a 'Beetle Boat' on the island of Culebra in Puerto Rico in 1923. The 'Beetle Boat' had been used by the British and French at Gallipoli in World War I.

The Fleet Marine Force

The final force to emerge, whose organization had been proposed by BrigGen John H. Russell, MajGen Fuller's assistant, came closer to one brigade of infantry and supporting elements as opposed to the corps' level organization advanced by Army officers. BrigGen Russell, a Naval Academy graduate and a strong advocate in the maintenance of close ties with the Navy, proposed on 17 August of 1933 in a memorandum to the Chief of Naval Operations that the 'Marine Expeditionary Force' be discarded, and replaced by an entirely new organization called the 'Fleet Marine Force', abbreviated as FMF, which would be under the operational control of the Fleet Commander when embarked on the ships of the fleet or engaged in exercises afloat or ashore. In garrison, the FMF would remain under the administrative jurisdiction of the Major General Commandant.

Approved by MajGen Fuller, the Secretary of the Navy likewise placed his endorsement on BrigGen Russell's recommendations, and on 8 December 1933 the Navy Department codified the FMF with General Order 241, which charged the Commandant of the Marine Corps 'to submit proposed instructions for establishing appropriate command and administrative relations between the com-mander in chief and the commander of the Fleet Marine Force.' Besides establishing the command relationship of the FMF, General Order 241 outlined the specific duties of this new organization in that 'it shall constitute a part of the organization of the United States Fleet and be included in the operating force plan for each year'. As for the strength of this force, the Navy Department maintained that the Fleet Marine Force shall 'consist of such units as may be designated by the Major General Commandant and shall be maintained at such strength as is warranted by the general personnel situation of the Marine Corps.'

Slow Progress

Organization of the FMF was, needless to say, slow. MajGen Russell, who replaced MajGen Fuller as Commandant of the Marine Corps, wrote in his annual report for 1934, that the size of the FMF for that year was 'approximately 3000

Deploying from column into echelon and line abreast. The four-man section was the smallest fighting unit of the US Marines. Note that the BAR-equipped Marine remains in a position to give fire support against a threat from any side.

Above: A Christie 'amphibious tank' lands on Culebra during the US Marines' 1924 Winter Maneuvers. While the vehicle proved unseaworthy, it nonetheless served as the basis for further experiments with amphibious vehicles.

enlisted men, organized into one regiment of infantry, two batteries of 75mm pack howitzers, one battery of 155mm guns, one battery of .50 calibre anti-aircraft machine guns, and Aircraft One and Two (an observation and pursuit aviation squadron respectively).'

When MajGen Russell became Commandant of the Marine Corps in February 1934, the FMF remained under-strength, due largely to manpower shortages and austere budgets attributed to the cutbacks in military spending in the 1930s. MajGen Russell lamented in his first annual report to the Secretary of the Navy that 'The remaining component units of the Fleet Marine Force, namely, two regiments of infantry, three battalions 6" guns, and four battalions anti-aircraft, cannot be maintained even in a skeletonized status.' Nonetheless, the FMF participated in manoeuvres with the fleet off of San Clemente, CA, and in the Caribbean areas, and the headquarters transferred from Quantico, VA, to Marine Corps Base, San Diego, as Marines continued to train and officers returned to the classrooms, to codify in manual form a workable landing doctrine that served as a primer for the amphibious assaults undertaken during World War II. Furthermore, with an end to the US

occupation of Haiti, and an increase in the Corps' strength, by 1935 HQMC was able to organize two Marine brigades for the FMF, with one on the east coast, stationed at the Marine Barracks, Quantico, and the other headquartered at the Marine Corps Base, San Diego.

As more manpower became available, the FMF went from primarily a 'paper' organization to a fully-fledged fighting force, guided as always by the ideas laid down at the Marine Corps Schools, with the formulation of the *Tentative Landing Manual* (1934), which became the 'bible' for the conduct of amphibious assault. The basic tenets of this landing manual, established by a board of Marine officers specially appointed by MajGen Fuller in 1930–31, set forth in detail, during the 1933–34 school term at the Field Officers Course, Quantico, VA, the doctrines and techniques to be followed both in training and during actual landing operations. After several major revisions in both content and title, the *Tentative Landing Manual* became the 'guide for forces of the Navy and Marine Corps conducting a landing against opposition'. In fact, the *Tentative Landing Manual* became, in time, the foundation of all amphibious warfare thinking in the United States Armed Forces. While the US Navy renamed this manual *Fleet Training Publication 167*, the US Army issued the same manual as *Field Manual 31-5*, which became its standard text used in all amphibious operations from North Africa to Normandy during World War II.

THE FLEET FORCE 1934
1 Regiment of Infantry
2 Batteries of 75mm (2.95in) Pack Howitzers
1 Battery of 155mm (6.1in) Howitzers
1 Battery of .50in (12.7mm) Calibre Anti-aircraft Guns
2 Squadrons – Aircraft One and Two
Aggregate Strength . . . . 3000 Marines

Above: US Marines land from 'whaleboats' and ships' boats during an early amphibious landing exercise at Quantico, Virginia, in the 1920s. In essence, the theory behind amphibious landings had changed little from the time of Wolfe's attack on Quebec in 1759.

The manual covered such topics as command relationships, naval gunfire support (authored by Navy Lieutenant Walter C. Ansel, one of the original board members at Quantico), combat loading and unloading, and the creation of shore parties. The shore party was a special task organization, headed by a beachmaster designated to organize the beach area in order to locate logistical sites, and other support equipment, as well as the movement of the same inland. While many of the principles outlined in these various topics remained untested and purely theoretical, the Marines, Navy, and eventually Army nonetheless held manoeuvres, where they learned and relearned many valuable lessons not covered by the manual. These proved extremely valuable when the first amphibious assaults by US forces took place on Guadalcanal and later in North Africa.

TACTICAL ORGANIZATION AND TRAINING IN THE 1930S

The standard combat formation of the US Marine Corps during the interwar period was the rifle regiment, which had normally two battalions, with each battalion made up of three rifle companies of three platoons each. Each battalion had an attached machine gun and mortar company that consisted of one mortar platoon and three machine gun platoons. Armament for the mortar and machine gun company included the World War I-era M1917 Browning .30in (7.62mm) calibre water-cooled machine guns, and 81mm (3.2in) mortars. Marines pulled the machine guns with additional ammunition on a Cole machine gun cart. Enlisted Marines carried the .30in (7.62mm) calibre, bolt-action M1903 Springfield rifle that weighed (3.94kg (8.69lb), and had a maximum effective range of 549m (600yd); could fire ten rounds per minute, and penetrate 6.35mm (.25in) steel plating at that same range. Those Marines designated as automatic riflemen carried the .30in (7.62mm) calibre Browning Automatic Rifle or 'BAR', which was fed by a 20-round magazine. The BAR could fire in either the automatic or semi-automatic mode, and had a maximum effective range of 549m (600yd), though seldom engaged enemy targets at such a long range. Fired in short or long bursts, the BAR could fire anywhere from 350 to 550 rounds per minute, though the semi-automatic mode was preferred, with short bursts at a rate of about 125 to 150 rounds per minute. Besides the bayonet issued along with the service rifle, and hand grenades, other weapons carried by Marines, primarily officers and noncommissioned officers, was the M1911 .45in (11.4mm) automatic pistol, which had a magazine that carried seven rounds, a maximum range of 1463m (1600yd) and an effective range of 23m (25yd), as well as the Thompson submachine gun, used extensively and very effectively in the jungles of Nicaragua. As for the uniforms of the Marines during this period, they wore a khaki shirt and trousers along with, in garrison, a campaign hat with the Marine Corps emblem or, in the field, the World War I-era steel helmet.

Insofar as training was concerned, in garrison Marines attended classes in the mornings on rifle marksmanship, first aid, weapons nomenclature and maintenance, and close order drill, and in the afternoon played sports. When in the field, the leathernecks conducted small unit (company and battalion) patrols, constructed weapons emplacements, and performed manoeuvres, as well as long conditioning hikes throughout the Virginia countryside, and hills surrounding San Diego. Marine aviators flew and continued to hone their skills at aerial gunnery, bombing, and strafing runs. Despite the limited budgets of the era, Marines continued to train and train hard.

Deployments: The 1930s

During the 1930s, as the writing of the *Tentative Landing Manual* went forward, the 4th Marines remained on duty in Shanghai and Tientsin (Tianjin), guarding the International Settlement, protecting American and foreign citizens, and the US Consulate in Peking. The Marine Legation Detachment, referred to as the 'Horse Marines', famous for its smart looks, rode in many ceremonial parades and drilled whilst mounted on its small, sturdy Mongolian ponies, and in time became a part of the colourful legacy of the so-called 'China Marines' during this period. In 1938 HQMC sent additional forces to Shanghai to reinforce the 4th Marines after the outbreak of war between China and Japan in 1937. Other Marine detachments stood duty on Guam in the Marianas; in the Territory of Hawaii, and at the

THE FLEET MARINE FORCE 1935
1st Marine Brigade, FMF, Quantico, VA.
Headquarters Company, 1st Marine Brigade
5th Marines (less 3rd Bn)
1st Bn, 10th Marines (75mm (2.95in) pack howitzers)
1st Chemical Company
1st Engineer Company
1st Tank Company, (Marmon-Harrington light tank)
Battery 'B' 15th Marines (Anti-aircraft)
Aircraft One
St. Thomas, Virgin Islands
VMS-3 Squadron (Aviation)
2nd Marine Brigade, FMF, San Diego, CA.
Headquarters, 2nd Brigade, FMF
Headquarters Company, 2nd Marine Brigade
6th Marines (less 3rd Bn)
2nd Bn, 10th Marines (75mm (2.95in) pack howitzers)
2nd Chemical Company
2nd Engineer Company
2Bn, Battery 'F' 15th Marines (Anti-aircraft)
Aircraft Two

US Naval Base at Guantanamo Bay, Cuba. During political unrest in Cuba in 1933, President Franklin D. Roosevelt ordered the Atlantic Fleet to concentrate in Cuban waters with an attached Marine force, which temporarily suspended the ongoing organization of the FMF.

The Fleet Marine Force, 1933–1941

Besides the emphasis on landing operations, Marine aviators were likewise busy refining the techniques of close-in air support for the infantry on the ground, as well as in pursuit tactics and aerial resupply. Absorbing the lessons learned in Haiti, the Dominican Republic, and especially Nicaragua, Marine aviators, equipped with faster, more sturdier monoplanes and training with both US Army aviators at Kelley Field, Texas, and with the Navy at Pensacola, Florida, soon became an important component in the development of amphibious warfare theory then underway at the Marine Corps Schools at Quantico. In early 1931, the first carrier-based Marine squadron joined the USS *Lexington*, an arm of the Marines that in time would become an important adjunct to the prosecution of a naval air campaign to support amphibious assaults.

Much of the focus of the Corps during the 1930s was on the ongoing development of the FMF and amphibious warfare. As Europe drifted slowly towards war in the mid-to-late 1930s with the rise of Adolf Hitler and the Nazis in Germany

Below: US Marines in action in Haiti in 1918–20. In fighting in the so-called 'Banana Wars' of the interwar era, the Marines learned many valuable lessons that they later used to good effect in the South Pacific during World War II.

Above: A US Marine Staff Sergeant instructs a recruit in the proper position to fire a Thompson sub-machine gun in the late 1930s. The Thompson proved extremely popular as a weapon, giving Marines much greater individual firepower than the M1 carbine.

in 1933, and the 'incidents' that occurred between Japan and China on the Asian mainland from 1931 with an ever-growing frequency, US military planners began to re-examine their warfighting strategy, despite the continuing effects of the Great Depression on the US and its military, and the country's isolationist non-interventionist foreign policies.

As Europe went to war on 1 September 1939, the US Marine Corps continued to conduct landing exercises to test its doctrines with a greater sense of urgency, and enjoyed a slight increase in manpower from 15,000 to 17,000 officers and men in 1937, putting the Corps on a firm foundation as its senior leaders laid the groundwork for the eventual World War II expansion that began in earnest in 1940. In order to secure more funding and manpower, MajGen Thomas Holcomb, Marine Corps Commandant (1936–1943), sought to increase the strength of the Marine Corps Reserve by instituting a more rigorous training schedule, with mandatory drills and a two-week summer camp for reservists, as well as integrating the Regular and Reserve Officer Corps' training program at Quantico to ensure that when war came, the reserve would become an important source of available manpower to augment the FMF. MajGen Holcomb, a veteran of World War I, and former director of training at headquarters, emphasized the need for training and integration of combat teams of infantry and artillery with air support, and increased liaison and communication between the various arms. Training during this period increased in tempo and complexity, with field problems that emphasized brigade-level problems and tactical inspections by brigade commanders to ensure readiness.

The Defense Battalions

As the FMF evolved into a full-fledged fighting force, HQMC made tactical formations to accommodate these changes. MajGen Holcomb, ever mindful of the isolationist sentiments of the country, though aware of the manpower shortages that still plagued the Marine Corps, came up with a solution to win congressional approval for an increase in the size of the Corps yet retain an outward appearance of increasing only the defensive potential of the Marines. Admiral William D. Leahy suggested to Holcomb that his request for additional men and material be earmarked for the Advanced Base or Base Defense Force. In keeping with the defensive aspects of this Advanced Base Force, HQMC designed an entirely new force that kept within the parameters of a purely defensive mission with no offensive capability – the Base Defense Force. By June 1940, the Commandant of the Marine Corps was able to report to the Secretary of the Navy in his annual report that four defense battalions had been organized and trained, as well as having received permission to organize two more, a total of six. The development of the defense battalions gave the Marine Corps a balanced force 'designed to accomplish the seizure and securing of bases for the Fleet'. The defense battalions consisted of seacoast and anti-aircraft artillery batteries, searchlight and sound locator units, and anti-aircraft and beach defence machine gun units. While the strength of the defense battalions fluctuated, dependent upon 'the type of equipment furnished and will be prescribed by the Commandant from time to time', the normal composition of one of these units consisted of a headquarters and service battery, and a 90mm (3.54in) or 3in (76.2mm) AA group; additional strength came from either an attached 155mm (6.1in) artillery group, a special weapons group, 5in (127mm) artillery group, machine gun group, or a 7in (177.8mm) artillery group. The total strength of a defense battalion averaged between 1146 and 1196 Marines, dependent primarily upon the addition of a 155mm (6.1in) Artillery Group, a 90mm (3.54in) or 3in (76.2mm) Antiaircraft Group, and a Special Weapons Group.

As the war progressed from a defensive phase (1941–1943) to an offensive phase by 1944, the need for manpower and the artillery and anti-aircraft guns possessed by the defense battalions witnessed the gradual reduction and eventual conversion of these units into anti-aircraft units.

The Marine Division

During World War II, the Marine Division underwent many changes, perhaps the most important being the formation of a Marine Division itself! Prior to World War II, the largest Marine tactical formation was the brigade. During World

War I, two Marine brigades served in France, with the 4th Brigade engaging in extensive combat action from Belleau Wood in the Chateau Thierry, Saint Mihiel, Marbache, and in the Meuse Argonne offensives late in the war. Both General John J. Pershing, the American Expeditionary Forces' commanding officer, and the War Department refused MajGen Commandant George Barnett's repeated request to form a Marine Division. By war's end in 1918, the Marines had sufficient manpower to form such a division, though the armistice ended any further need for such a large Marine outfit, and the remaining Marines in the United States returned to routine garrison duty or expeditionary duty in Haiti and the Dominican Republic.

A Marine brigade normally consisted of two Marine regiments, a machine gun battalion divided between the two regiments, a supply and headquarters company, and a battalion of artillery. With the formation of the FMF, an 'embryonic' division began to take shape, with the formation of more permanent units that were 'expandable', that is created with the direct intention that they could be formed into larger tactical organizations if necessary.

The first Marine Division, formed out of the 1st Brigade, then stationed throughout the east coast of the United States, concentrated at the Marine Barracks, New River, North Carolina, which gave Marines a suitable and much larger training base where they could train their newly-created amphibious assault forces. In honor of the thirteenth commandant of the Marine Corps, MajGen John A. Lejeune, who had been a forceful advocate of the advanced base mis-

sion during the 1920s, and an amphibious warfare pioneer, the Marine Corps renamed the New River Base – Camp Lejeune, NC.

The result of this concentration was the formation of the 1st Marine Division, that had a strength by July 1942 (prior to its landing on Guadalcanal, in the Solomons, on 7 August 1942) of 19,514 Marines, comprised of 865 commissioned officers and 16,987 enlisted Marines, with 115 commissioned and 1547 Naval personnel (medical officers, corpsmen, and naval construction teams known as 'Seabees').

Throughout World War II, the Marine division retained its triangular basis of three infantry regiments, with each regiment containing three battalions of three companies each. Additional support came from an attached weapons company to each battalion that had a 20mm (.78in) anti-aircraft and anti-tank platoon, a 81mm (3.2in)mortar platoon, and three machine gun platoons. During the landing on Guadalcanal, the 20mm anti-aircraft gun was replaced by the 37mm (1.45in) anti-tank gun that broke up many Japanese banzai attacks. Additional firepower for each regiment came from an attached weapons company with a 75mm (2.95in) pack howitzer, with an attached anti-aircraft and anti-tank platoon.

Rifle companies consisted of three rifle platoons, a 60mm (2.36in) mortar section, and a light machine gun company. A

Below: Two US Marines man a Browning .30in (7.62mm) water-cooled heavy machine gun on Guadalcanal during the defence of Henderson Airfield during World War II. The Browning was an excellent weapon, if a little cumbersome for use in the field.

A US MARINE DIVISION JULY 1942 'D' SERIES

Headquarters Battalion and Headquarters Company *3031*
Special Troops
Signal Company
Military Police Company
Special Weapons Battalion
Headquarters and Service Battery
- 40mm (1.57in) Anti-aircraft Battery
- 90mm (3.54in) Anti-aircraft Battery
- 3 Anti-tank Batteries
Parachute Battalion
Headquarters Company
3 Parachute Companies
Tank Battalion (Light)
Headquarters Company
Scout Company
3 Tank Companies

Service Troops *1946*
Service Battalion
Headquarters Company
Service and Supply Company
Ordnance Company
Division Transport Company
3 Regimental Transport Companies
Medical Battalion
Headquarters and Service Company
5 Medical Companies
Amphibian Tractor Battalion
Headquarters and Service Company
3 Amphibian Tractor Companies

Engineer Regiment *2454*
Headquarters and Service Company
Engineer Battalion
3 Engineer Companies
Pioneer Battalion
Headquarters Company
3 Pioneer Companies
Naval Construction Battalion ('Seabees')*
Headquarters Company
3 Construction Companies

Artillery Regiment *2581*
Headquarters and Service Battery
105mm Howitzer Battalion
Headquarters and Service Battery
3 105mm (4.13in) Howitzer Batteries
3 75mm (2.95in) Pack Howitzer Battalions
Headquarters and Service Battery
3 75mm (2.95in) Pack Howitzer Batteries

3 Infantry Regiments *9504*
Headquarters and Service Company
Weapons Company**
3 Infantry Battalions
Headquarters Company
Weapons Company***
3 Rifle Companies****

Total Strength of a Marine Division (1942):
19,516 officers and enlisted men

*   The versatility of the Seabees is reflected by the composition of each construction company, which had: a maintenance and operations platoon; two construction platoons, a road blasting and excavation platoon, a waterfront platoon, and a tanks, steel, and pipe platoon.

**   The regimental weapons company consisted of a company headquarters, a 75mm (2.95in) gun platoon, and an anti-aircraft and anti-tank platoon.

***   The battalion weapons company consisted of a company headquarters, a 20mm (.78in) anti-aircraft and anti-tank platoon, an 81mm (3.18in) mortar platoon, and three machine gun platoons. The D-Series Tables and Equipment (T/E) specified that when the 20mm dual-purpose gun was not available, the 37mm (1.45in) gun was to be substituted, which was fortunate, for the Marines employed this weapon with good effect throughout the war.

****Each rifle company had a company headquarters, a weapons platoon (consisting of 60mm mortar section and a light machine gun section), and three rifle platoons. The rifle platoon was broken down into a platoon headquarters, a BAR squad, and three rifle squads.

platoon consisted of three rifle squads, a Browning Automatic Rifle (BAR) squad, and platoon headquarters. HQMC adopted this triangular concept due to its ability to provide the maximum amount of firepower to infantry commanders during a landing or attack inland from the beachhead. It proved very effective in reducing Japanese defences during the Central Pacific drive (November 1943–September 1944), particularly on Tarawa in the Gilbert Islands, and later on Saipan in the Marianas in mid-1944.

The Marine division went through two modifications during the war. Due to the changing tempo of the war, HQMC recognized need to make the division a more effec-tive and flexible fighting machine. The E-Series Marine Division, officially designated on 15 April 1943, increased in strength, with the addition of 451 sailors and Marines, with a simultaneous reduction taking place with the transfer of the parachute battalion, and reduction in the size of the special weapons, light tank, and service battalions. At the same time, HQMC placed the three regimental transport companies into a composite motor transport battalion with the addition of 84 more Marines and 130 vehicles, while the engineer and rifle regiments each received an additional 100 men. The artillery regiment expanded to include an additional 105mm (4.1in) howitzer battalion.

Due to the experiences of the fighting on Tarawa and for the upcoming assault on the Marianas and Ryukus, HQMC once again authorized a change in the division structure. The F-Series Marine Division, officially designated on 5 May 1944, had 2500 less men that its predecessor, with the disbandment of the special weapons battalion, a reduction in division service troops, and the transfer of the amphibian tractor battalion to corps troops. The light tank battalion became an independent battalion, reduced in strength to 594 Marines, with the loss of its scout company which HQMC attached to the division and placed under the direct command of the division commander himself as a reconnaissance company, made up primarily of former Marine paratroopers and raiders. The engineer and pioneer battalions were likewise separated and formed into independent entities within a Marine division. Due to their constant service and demands elsewhere the Naval Construction Battalions (Seabees) headquarters detached them from the organic structure of a division though re-attached them as a component part of the landing force in assault landings. As for the artillery regiment, it now consisted of two 75mm (2.95in) pack howitzer battalions and two 105mm (4.1in) howitzer battalions. While the Marine artillery regiment was considerably lighter than its Army counterpart, due mainly to the amphibious nature of a Marine division, and lacking the addition of another 105mm howitzer battalion and 155mm (6.1in) howitzer battalion, it did have the service of heavier artillery which came from corps artillery.

Changes with the Regiment

While the last change made to the Marine divisional structure officially occurred at the end of World War II, many of the changes of the G-Series Marine Division affected primarily the infantry regiment, though it might be added that many of the changes in this organization occurred prior to the assault on Okinawa, with the addition of a 55-man assault platoon per regimental headquarters specially-equipped with flamethrowers, BARs, and demolition charges. Likewise, a 105mm howitzer platoon replaced the 75mm pack howitzer platoon just in time for the Okinawa invasion, and 'proved to be of inestimable value in the cave warfare' on that island.

Of all the organic assets not reduced in all the series of divisional changes was that of the Marine regiment, which consistently grew with the appearance of each succeeding table of organization. Company strength in the 1942

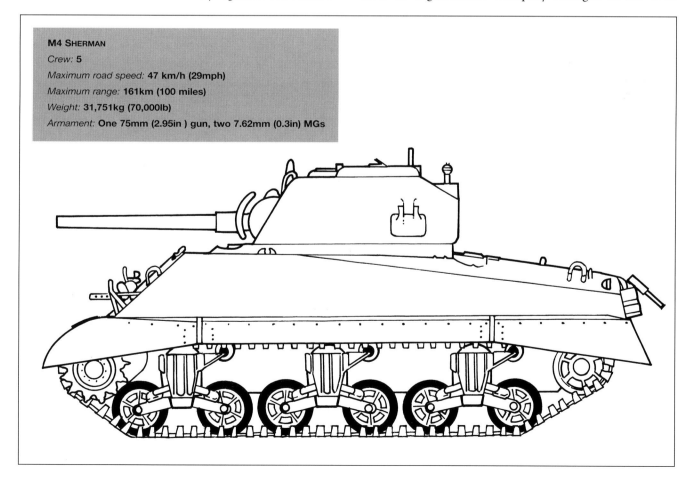

M4 SHERMAN

Crew: **5**

Maximum road speed: **47 km/h (29mph)**

Maximum range: **161km (100 miles)**

Weight: **31,751kg (70,000lb)**

Armament: **One 75mm (2.95in) gun, two 7.62mm (0.3in) MGs**

Above: A platoon of US Marines in action on Bougainville in mid-1943. Note the newly-adopted semi-automatic M1 Garand rifles carried by the most of the Marines, replacing the veteran M1903 Springfield rifles.

D-Series was 183; 196 in the E-Series; 235 in the F-Series; and 242 in the G-Series. This increase in the size of the regiment was due primarily to the fact that the 'machine gun platoon [44 men in 1944, 56 in 1945] was added to the rifle company in order to offset the loss of the weapons platoon', which was merely lost administratively and not in actuality. In fact, with the transfer of the 60mm (2.36in) mortar section to the company HQ, rifle companies actually gained four men with the addition of the 44-man machine gun platoon.

Rifle Companies, Platoons, and Squads

The fighting in the Pacific during World War II was a war fought in dense jungles, as well as on rough, rocky, coral terrain that often prohibited the movement of large units as in North Africa, in Russia, or in northwestern Europe. It was a conflict fought largely by small units, from rifle companies, platoons to squads and fire teams. For the US Marine Corps, these formations became the primary tactical units

that 'closed with by fire and maneuver' against the Japanese on the many atolls and jungles of the Central and Southwest Pacific. In fact, the nature of the fighting in the Pacific placed greater emphasis on the tactical as opposed to the operational art of war, and in many instances this held the difference between victory or defeat. Here, the Marine Corps' experience in Nicaragua and in Hispaniola during the interwar period in small unit operations paid large dividends in terms of the tactical lessons learned and re-learned as they battled the Japanese from island to island.

The Marine rifle company, made up of three rifle platoons with a weapons platoon, was the primary tactical unit in the Pacific War. Broken down into raw figures, the D-Series rifle platoon had 42 Marines in a platoon headquarters of 7 men, an 8-man automatic rifle (BAR) squad, and three 9-man squads. The automatic rifle (BAR) squad consisted of a squad leader armed with a submachine gun (Thompson), two BAR men, and five riflemen trained to assume the duties of an automatic rifleman if necessary. Initially, these five riflemen did not appear in the tables of organization, though in subsequent reorganizations of the rifle platoon HQMC added them directly into the fighting strength of a platoon and company. In 1942, a rifle squad consisted of a squad leader, a BAR rifleman, six riflemen who carried the M1903 .30in (7.62mm) calibre bolt-action 'Springfield' (replaced in April 1943 with the M-1 Garand), and rifle grenadier, armed with a Springfield rifle with an attached grenade launcher. In short, a 1942 D-Series Marine Division had the fighting strength of 5285 carbines, 7962 rifles with additional firepower coming from Browning water-cooled machine guns, light and heavy mortars, and light machine guns.

With the tempo of the fighting in the Central Pacific becoming increasingly bitter, the necessity for added firepower led to the dropping of the BAR squad with the addition of a third rifle squad, which in turn increased in strength to twelve Marines: squad leader, assistant squad leader, six riflemen, and two assistant BAR men, all armed with M-1s, and two BAR men. This gave balance and firepower to each 6-man squad that now had a BAR attached to it.

Further Squad Changes

Prior to the start of the campaign in the Marshall and Marianas Islands (January–September 1944), changes once again occurred in the rifle squad, with the creation of three four-man fire teams, each one supported by a BAR man, and led by a fire team leader. This not only permitted greater tactical flexibility, but brought about an equal distribution of additional firepower to bear for the squad in attack. These changes, incorporated into the F-Series Rifle Squad after a year long study at the Marine Corps Schools in March 1944, saw an increase of the squad from 12 to 13 Marines. This new squad consisted of a squad leader armed with an M-1 carbine, three fire team leaders and three riflemen armed with M-1s and M-7 grenade launchers, three

---

Below: A well-armed Marine assault team climbs over a destroyed
Japanese position during the fighting on Okinawa during April
1945. These teams proved very effective in dislodging the
Japanese from their reinforced bunkers.

assistant BAR men armed with carbines and M-8 grenade launchers, and three BAR men. After the campaign at Cape Gloucester, the fire team standardized with a fire team leader, rifleman, BAR man, and assistant BAR man, and this remained intact until the end of the war.

The changes made in the composition and concept of employment of the rifle squad, as well as to the combat principles underlying the organization of the fire team 'were a culmination of Marine tactical experience to that time'. This 'fire team' concept of employment not only provided for great delegation of command authority to squad and fire team leaders, it also allowed for better tactical manoeuvreability and aggressive employment of a squad and platoon's weapons in the achievement of a tactical objective. In short, with the creation of the three 4-man fire teams, the squad leader could better direct his fire team leaders to manoeuvre their firepower as whole units against enemy positions. Other benefits of the fire team concept were: maintenance of mutual support in the defence; decentralization of fire control; decentralization of command; mobility; flexibility; rapid absorption of replacements during reorganization under combat conditions; the adaptability to special training and the accomplishment of missions involving the employment of special equipment.

Paramarines, Raiders, and Reconnaissance Marines

As the US Marine Corps rushed to mobilise its forces for possible combat, it began experimenting with two unique formations that captivated Marines, though had little intrinsic value to the overall fighting during World War II. These were the parachute and raider battalions, organized largely as a result of the German airborne operations on Crete and during the campaign for the Low Countries in April–May 1940, and from the experiences of LtCol Evans F. Carlson with the Chinese Communist Eighth Route Army during the Chinese Civil War in 1934.

The organization of the first parachute battalion in the US Marine Corps began in October 1940, as the first group of leatherneck jumpers assembled at the Lakehurst, New Jersey, naval training station and later at Quantico, VA, in May 1941, with another battalion, the 2nd, having been formed at Camp Elliott, San Diego, CA. As mobilization continued, the East Coast Parachute Battalion moved its operations to first, New River, NC, and later joined up with its sister battalion at Camp Gillespie, CA, the permanent home of Marine parachutists who trained there from June 1941 to early 1944, when HQMC disbanded and merged them with existing rifle regiments. Organized into the 1st

Left: A Paramarine displays his camouflaged parachute on Bougainville in mid-1943. While no Paramarine unit jumped into battle, they did fight on land as reconnaissance troops. Much of the terrain the Marines fought over was unsuitable for large-scale landings.

Parachute Regiment, the paratroopers who belonged to this regiment saw action on Tulagi and later on Guadalcanal, and New Georgia (Choiseul) in October 1943. While the parachutists performed valuable yeoman service on Choiseul by diverting the attention of the Japanese away from the main landings on Bougainville, they proved to be too lightly armed to deal with the Japanese troops they went up against. Likewise, a shortage of lift aircraft to carry them into battle forced HQMC to disband the Paramarines in December 1943, when they became the nucleus of the newly-formed Fifth Marine Division.

The second 'special' unit organized by HQMC that has received much attention by historians were the Raiders of the First and Second Battalions. The 1st Marine Raider Battalion, formed from the 1st Bn, 5th Marines, and commanded by LtCol Merritt A. Edson, organized at Quantico, VA, and landed on Tulagi, Gavutu, Tanambogo, and the Florida Islands where it became involved, according to Sergeant James Smith, one of the original members of the 1st Raider Bn, in a bitter fight with the Japanese who had retreated into a labyrinth of caves armed with machine guns well-concealed behind sandbags and other obstacles. When the fighting shifted from Tulagi to nearby Guadalcanal, the members of the 1st Raiders saw extensive action on the main island of Guadalcanal, where on the night of 12–13 September they repulsed a large scale Japanese attack on what is now known as 'Bloody' or 'Edson's' Ridge. In subsequent fighting on Guadalcanal, the Raiders of the 1st Battalion distinguished themselves in the fighting that oftentimes was bloody and hand-to-hand.

The other Raider battalion, the 2nd, commanded by LtCol Evans F. Carlson, who had witnessed the Chinese Civil War, and accompanied Mao Zedong's Eighth Route Army into the mountains on its 'Long March' as a military observer for HQMC, likewise saw extensive fighting. With the support of President Franklin D. Roosevelt, and the President's son, James Jr, himself a Marine major and Carlson's executive officer, LtCol Carlson built the 2nd Raider Battalion into a highly effective combat organization that conducted raids on Makin in the Gilbert Islands (17 August 1942), and later served on Guadalcanal, harassing the Japanese and disrupting their communications that prevented them from effectively reinforcing their frontline troops. In fact, for nearly thirty days, (4 November–4 December 1940) the Raiders of Carlson's 2nd Battalion conducted a 241km (150 mile) combat and reconnaissance patrol over some of the roughest terrain, and killed an estimated 500 Japanese troops, while losing only 16 men to enemy action.

Eventually, HQMC organized the 3rd (LtCol Harry B. Liversedge), and 4th (Major James L. Roosevelt) Raider Battalions which, when merged with the 1st and 2nd Battalions became the 1st Raider Regiment and saw action on New Georgia, while the 2nd Raider Regiment (organized in September 1943), went into combat on Bougainville. Like the Paramarines, however, the Raiders were too lightly armed (the heaviest weapon being the 60mm (2.36in) mortar), and though eventually employed for the intended purpose of their organization in raids and reconnaissance missions, HQMC eventually disbanded both the Raiders and Paramarines and organized both regiments into the reconstituted 4th Marine Regiment.

The last special unit organized by the Marines was a reconnaissance company formed as a result of the experiences of Colonel William J. Whaling's scout-sniper groups on Guadalcanal. Many of the Marines assigned to this permanent formation came, in fact, from the Raider and parachute battalions, which were eventually disbanded in favour of strengthening existing Marine rifle battalions and regiments. Travelling by foot, rubber rafts or jeeps, the job of these reconnaissance company Marines was to scout and patrol and, in effect, became the 'eyes and ears' of the divisional commanders. In this particular unit, Marine commanders placed infantry skills at a premium as they fanned out throughout the battlefield in search of enemy units and positions.

Special Assault Detachments

As a result of the fighting on Tarawa and the stiffening of Japanese resistance elsewhere in the Pacific, the changes made in the Marine division witnessed an increase in flame-throwers and demolition equipment issued, intended to strengthen the assault capabilities of Marine squads in dealing with an enemy that adopted the principles of interlocking and mutually-supporting defensive networks, not to mention the fanatical 'to-the death' principles that Japanese commanders adhered to after Guadalcanal. As the war moved increasingly closer to the Japanese mainland, the bitterness in the fighting increased proportionately. In fact, as the war progressed, both the US Marines and Army discovered that they were now up against an enemy determined to fight to the death and, in that regard, it became apparent to HQMC that this challenge would have to be met with the addition of enhanced firepower to deal with the increasing resistance.

Thus, the number of flamethrowers and demolition charges increased in the Marine Corps' Division's Tables of Equipment. While Marine rifle squads had flamethrowers and bazookas, as well as dynamite and other demolition charges, available to them on an as needed basis, the assault on Tarawa demonstrated that, unlike the fighting on Guadalcanal and in the northern Solomons (Bougainville and New Georgia in 1943), the Marines were facing an entirely new war against an old foe.

In fact, it was on Tarawa that the concept of 'find'em, fix'em, and blast'em' became axiomatic in Marine terminology. On Tarawa, Marine combat units pioneered the concept called the 'corkscrew method' in dealing with pillboxes and machine gun nests, where squads first isolated them and then, under the cover of heavy volumes of rifle and machine gun fire, blasted the emplacements with bazookas and demolition charges, and then sprayed them with flamethrowers. During the fighting on Peleliu, arguably one of the costliest and perhaps most unnecessary amphibious assaults during the island-hopping campaign in the Pacific, 'Marines had at their disposal a 60-man assault platoon formed from a battalion's rifle companies, armed with flame-throwers and bazookas to deal with the interlocking defences built into that island's natural defensive terrain'.

The G-Series Division

With the lessons from the Peleliu and later Iwo Jima campaigns, where Marines encountered fanatical resistance unlike anything encountered elsewhere in the Pacific or in Europe for that matter, the new G-Series Table of Organization reflected the fact that rifle companies could not

Below: Marine 'Raiders' disembark from a transport into awaiting rubber rafts in late 1942 in order to launch a raid or conduct a reconnaissance on a Japanese-held island. The rubber vessels and their passengers were extremely vulnerable to hostile fire.

be stripped of available manpower to form special weapons platoons, with the addition of a 55-man assault platoon comprised of a platoon headquarters and three assault sections of two seven-man squads each. Each squad contained a squad leader, a flamethrower operator and his assistant, a bazooka operator and his assistant, and two demolition men. While this cut the available strength of flamethrowers from 27 to 12, there was now a trained unit to be exclusively utilized in the destruction of enemy strongpoints, thus allowing a rifle squad to continue uninterrupted in the assault.

The changes made throughout the fighting in the Pacific in the organizational structure of a Marine division reflected the flexibility that the founders of the Fleet Marine Force had conceptualised in the 1920s and 1930s. Due to the nature of the island campaigns in the Central and Southwest Pacific, the US Marine Corps adapted its force structure to the geographical and tactical situations that the nature of the fighting presented. This can be seen from the first landings on Guadalcanal in August 1942, through to the invasion of Okinawa on 1 April 1945, as the Marine divisions added new tactical formations while dropping old ones that had outlived their usefulness. In a large sense, the island war was a giant laboratory of experimentation with individual units, that allowed the adoption or elimination of units as the tactical

situation changed throughout the Pacific campaign. In retrospect, 'each successive T/O change served to make the World War II Marine Division the most effective and deadliest amphibious assault unit in history to that time'.

In sum, much of the flexibility in a Marine division can be attributed to the US Marine Corps' participation in World War I and its introduction to modern warfare throughout the summer and fall of 1918 when, after that conflict, through experimentation and many trials and errors, Marine leaders concluded that any amphibious assault would have to be supported by fire and manoeuvre. By inculcating and experimenting whenever they could during the 1920s and 1930s, Marines put to good use the lessons of World War I in their amphibious assaults during the campaigns in the Central and Southwest Pacific. In turn, the lessons in force structure and weapons deployment, when combined with the evolving doctrinal concepts of amphibious assault formed during the interwar period, made possible the emergence of the Marine Corps as a major component of the US Armed Forces in the second half of the twentieth century.

The evolution of the advanced base force from its origins in 1903 to the formation of the Fleet Marine Force in 1933 came about as a result of much trial and error, due largely to the efforts of such men as Major Generals John A. Lejeune,

M1903 SPRINGFIELD *Calibre:* **7.62mm (0.3in);** *Length:* **1.105m (43.5in);** *Weight:* **4.1kg (9lb);** *Magazine:* **5-round box;** *System of operation:* **bolt action;** *Muzzle velocity:* **855mps (2805ftps)**

M1 BAZOOKA *Calibre:* **60mm (2.36in);** *Length:* **1.384m (54.5in);** *Weight (launcher only):* **6.01kg (13.25lb);** *Weight (rocket):* **1.54kg (3.4lb);** *System of operation:* **Electrically fired;** *Muzzle velocity:* **83.2mps (270ftps)**

John. H. Russell, and Brigadier Generals Robert H. Dunlap and Eli K. Cole, as well as a host of other Marine officers and enlisted men who laboured on, despite budget and manpower cuts, in pioneering the concepts and doctrine of amphibious assault.

The emergence of the FMF came at a critical juncture in the institutional history of the US Marine Corps and the war planning process prior to World War II. As war clouds gathered over Europe and Asia in the 1930s, Marine planners struggled to convince a sceptical Navy and Army leadership that given proper equipment, combat support, and combat service support, the amphibious assault could succeed. Yet the doctrine they laid out in the *Tentative Landing Manual* of 1934 remained largely untested until the assault on Tarawa in the Gilbert Islands on 20 November 1943, which can be considered the first real amphibious 'assault' in the Pacific during World War II. It was on Tarawa that a reinforced Marine division came ashore in the face of murderous Japanese fire to seize, after three days of heavy fighting, an enemy-held island. On Tarawa, the Marines demonstrated what an amphibious landing required in terms of fire and logistics support, concepts that were only theoretical until put into practice in combat conditions. In fact, while historians have labelled the landing on Guadalcanal on 7 August 1942 the first amphibious assault of the war, the landings there more closely resembled an amphibious 'insertion', or the seizure and defence of an advanced naval base, instead of a forcible insertion that Marines employed later on in the Central Pacific.

Above: Elements of the 6th Marines land on D+1 on Tarawa in November 1943. Although landing craft and LVT amphibious vehicles were increasingly commonplace, the majority of Marines would get their feet wet, wading the last few metres to the shore.

As Marines moved across the Central Pacific, in a relentless drive to 'link up' with the forces of General Douglas MacArthur's Southwest Pacific Theater as they drove toward the liberation of the Philippine Islands, they discovered that the force structure that landed on Guadalcanal would have to be reinforced with increased firepower to dislodge an enemy that had built an elaborate system of defences and mutually-supporting positions to delay for as long as possible the assault on Japan. As the fighting grew closer to the Japanese mainland with the assault on Iwo Jima on 19 February 1945, and on Okinawa in April 1945, the changes in the organization and additional firepower of a Marine division not only increased its manoeuvreability but also its lethality, which proved to be not only critical to the successes it enjoyed, but vitally essential, as they came to grips with an enemy determined to fight to the death for every inch of Japanese soil. The flexibility in the tactical organization that permitted the US Marine Corps to 'experiment' with various formations during World War II came about largely as a result of the doctrinal debates of the 1920s and 1930s, as Marines strove to come up with a tactical and operational doctrine that gave both flexibility and manoeuvreability to a fleet commander in the prosecution of a naval campaign in time of war.

CHAPTER 2

The Doctrinal Challenge of Amphibious Landings 1920s & 1930s

> For the US Marine Corps, much of the interwar period was spent in establishing and refining a doctrine for amphibious landing operations. The new doctrine required new equipment, and new techniques, and these would not be fully tested in combat until the Guadalcanal campaign in 1942.

FOR US MARINE THEORISTS during the interwar period, the failure of the British, Australian, and New Zealand forces to successfully force a beachhead at Gallipoli in April 1915 during World War I held both a fascination as well as a challenge as they sat down to 'establish' a mission and a doctrine for that service at the conclusion of their involvement in the late war. While demobilization and austere budgets soon descended upon the US Armed Forces as the guns on the Western Front fell silent, forward-thinking Marines, such as Major Generals George Barnett, John A. Lejeune, as well as Colonels Robert H. Dunlap, Dion Williams, and one officer in particular – Major (later Lieutenant Colonel) Earl H. 'Pete' Ellis – evaluated and drew from both its previous advanced base exercises and experiences in World War I on how to best 're-direct' the Marine Corps toward a viable mission, as the expeditionary years quickly drew to a close in the Caribbean and Central America. They concluded that the Marine Corps' best interests and institutional survivability lay with the further development of its moribund advanced base force concept in the prosecution of a naval campaign. Most important, they saw the creation of a force and a doctrine that mutually supported

Left: A platoon of Marines wade through the surf to land on Cape Gloucester in December 1943, holding their M-1 carbines clear of the water to keep them dry. For them, months of intensive jungle fighting lay ahead.

and augmented the fighting forces called for in the Joint US Army and Navy Board's evolving War Plan 'Orange' (first promulgated in 1906).

Demobilization and a New, 'Old' Concept

Even as the guns fell silent on the Western Front in November 1918, the US Marine Corps slowly went from a force of 75,000 to approximately 23,000 officers and men, with the figure eventually dropping below that. Despite occupation duties in Germany at the war's conclusion, the Marine Corps returned to its traditional duties of providing sea-going ships' detachments, and men for the ongoing expeditions in the Dominican Republic and Haiti on the island of Hispaniola. The US Congress, after an intense lobbying effort by supporters of the Marines, passed into law an act, dated 11 July 1919, that authorized a corps of no more than 27,000 enlisted men. With a drop in wartime enthusiasm, however, the Marine Corps had barely been able to reach the 23,000-mark insofar as manpower had been concerned. Despite the decline in available manpower, both Major Generals Commandant George Barnett and his successor, John A. Lejeune, managed with some success the revival of the moribund Advanced Base Force. In fact, MajGen Barnett wrote in his annual report for 1919, despite the demobilization and discharge of the 'duration-of-war-Marines', that is, men who signed up for wartime service, 'the advanced base material and a skeletal organization have been retained, and the units of this will be reorganized as the men become

Above: Lieutenant Colonel Earl H. Ellis, author of *Advanced Base Operations in Micronesia: OPLAN 712 D*. He predicted how a war against Japan might be fought to a high degree of accuracy. He died mysteriously in 1923.

available'. This continued under MajGen Lejeune, who assumed command in June 1920, and moved the Advanced Base Force from Philadelphia to Quantico, VA, and renamed the force the Marine Corps Expeditionary Force (MCEF). Despite the constant demand for more Marines to be sent to Hispaniola, MajGen Lejeune sought to redirect the Marine Corps toward what he believed was its true mission: as an advanced base expeditionary force, that was to accompany the fleet in time of war, and be charged with the role of a base seizure and defence force. In the face of both demobilisation and austere budgets this proved to be, however, a daunting and formidable challenge.

Upon the assumption of office as the Major General Commandant of the Marine Corps, MajGen Lejeune began a thorough internal institutional reorganization and a realignment of Headquarters Marine Corps (HQMC) along modern staff lines, and realigned and reinvigorated the Marine Corps Schools (MCS) at Quantico. Meanwhile, as Lejeune continued his reforms inside the Marine Corps, representatives from the major powers convened in Washington,

DC, in the late autumn of 1920, to attend the Washington Naval Conference which had been called to begin the process of naval disarmament. As events transpired, this conference had significant consequences for the Marine Corps and the still-embryonic concept of amphibious assault.

The Washington Naval Conference

As the major naval powers of the United States, Great Britain, Japan, France, and Italy met to discuss a moratorium and eventual reduction in the number of capital ships constructed, the powers likewise discussed such issues as basing, overseas fortifications, and a treaty regarding China's territorial integrity. The main focus of the final treaty that emerged from the Washington Naval Conference that directly impacted on the Marine Corps were the clauses meant to appease the Japanese, who had been forced to reduce their naval tonnage in exchange for a pledge from the US that restricted the latter from fortifying its bases in the Philippines, and those west of the Hawaiian Island chain, particularly on the island of Guam in the Marianas. For her part, Great Britain likewise agreed not to fortify its naval bases at Singapore and Hong Kong. The major western powers also recognized Japan's mandates on the former German colonies in the Palau and Marshall Islands, given to her by the League of Nations for her declaration of war on Germany in the recently concluded World War I.

For American naval planners working within the framework of War Plan 'Orange', this meant that they would have to possibly 'seize, and defend' advanced base naval bases as they fought their way across the wide expanses of the Pacific. Major Earl H. Ellis, a brilliant, though erratic, staff officer, who had served as an operations officer with the 4th Marine Brigade, and a Lejeune favourite, undertook, while assigned to the Division of Operations and Training at HQMC, a major study of what the requirements of the Marine Corps would be in the event that war broke out between the US and the Japanese Empire. His work, published confidentially as *Advanced Base Operations in Micronesia, OPLAN 712-D* as an internal working document, became the Marine Corps' 'blueprint' in its preparation for its amphibious epic against Japan during World War II.

Major Ellis, using the Navy's War Plan 'Orange' as his guide, concluded in his study that from the outset of any naval war between the US and Japan, it can be assumed that the United States Navy would lose control of the Pacific Ocean, and the use of bases such as Guam and the Philippines. In essence, the US Navy and Army would then have to fight its way across the Pacific Ocean and retake these island possessions. Ellis held out the distinct possibility that the Japanese would fortify these same islands in the intervening period, in complete violation of the terms of the League of Nations mandates, thus requiring US forces to undertake a prolonged 'island-hopping' campaign to retake them.

For this campaign, the author of *OPLAN 712-D* concluded that because the Marine Corps was a part of the Navy, it would be the ideal force best suited to assist in what would surely be a naval campaign. Taking into account the technological advances of World War I, as well as forecasting the development of such things as landing craft and deadlier naval and aerial gunfire support, Maj Ellis believed that Marines, because of their training, and of the 'lessons learned' in World War I, could launch an amphibious assault, if well prepared from both the physical aspects as well as from a logistical standpoint.

Major Ellis, who had spent some time early in his career in the Philippines, had a long distrust of the Japanese, and parts of his study illustrated this very point. Furthermore, to 'prove' that the Japanese had violated the terms of the mandates assigned her by the League of Nations, he set out on a personal 'reconnaissance' of the Palau and Caroline Islands, where he had hoped to find the Japanese busily fortifying the islands. Major Ellis, disguised as an American business-

man, and officially 'on leave' from the Marine Corps, but with the full approval and knowledge of MajGen Lejeune, made several visits to these islands, where he found no visible sign of construction on the islands in question. Then, in what is still shrouded in mystery, despite the numerous articles and a recently published biography on the quixotic Ellis, the Marine major reportedly died of a liver or kidney ailment induced by an excessive intake of alcohol in the spring of 1923 on Palau. Despite the fact that Ellis found no unusual activity on the islands, the mysterious nature of his death and the brilliance of his amphibious warfighting plan prompted MajGen Lejeune to officially decree that *OPLAN-712* would 'henceforth be used as the basis for subsequent Marine Corps war planning and training.'

'WHALEBOATS AND TEXTBOOKS' 1920–1930

Fleet Exercises and the Marine Corps Schools

Even while LtCol Ellis (he had been advanced in grade posthumously) made his way across the Pacific, Marines had been busily experimenting with landing operations in the Caribbean on the Puerto Rican Island of Culebra, and near the locks of the Panama Canal. Marines soon

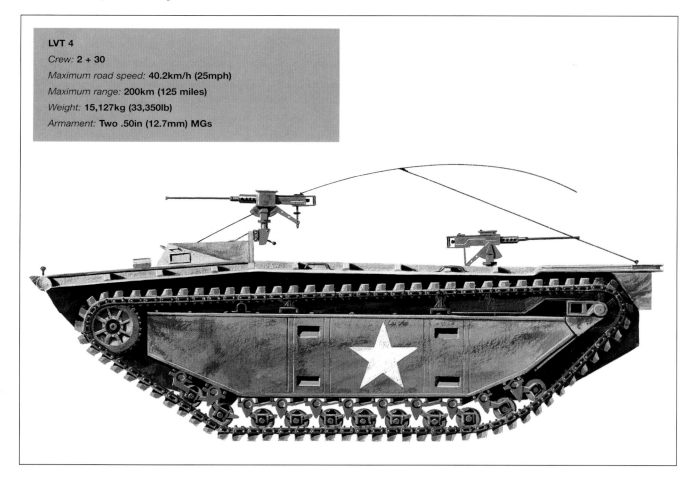

LVT 4

Crew: **2 + 30**

Maximum road speed: **40.2km/h (25mph)**

Maximum range: **200km (125 miles)**

Weight: **15,127kg (33,350lb)**

Armament: **Two .50in (12.7mm) MGs**

Above: Marines practice embarkation and disembarkation from a jetty at Quantico during the 1930s. Scramble nets would be hung over the side of the transport ship, and Marines would have to climb down into the boat – something that required a calm sea.

discovered that landing operations involved more than just putting troops in whaleboats and sending them ashore, and was, instead, a military science in itself. In fact, Marines discovered as these exercises commenced that they possessed neither suitable landing craft, nor a landing doctrine that could assist them in the identification of problems to be corrected. Yet it was the former problem, the lack of suitable landing craft, that initially hampered these postwar advanced base exercises. This, in fact, remained a major stumbling block that hampered planners at HQMC and the MCS as they sat down to wrestle with the problems of amphibious warfare up to the eve of World War II.

The Search for a Landing Craft

From the first postwar advanced base exercise in January–February 1922 up until the development of the 'Eureka', by boat builder Andrew Jackson Higgins in 1936, the primary concern and effort of the Marine Corps and the US Navy was to find a suitable landing craft capable of bringing men, artillery, and material ashore during a landing operation on a hostile beach. Both Navy and Marine officers looked at design after design, all to no avail, as a lack of funds during an era of austere military budgets stymied most attempts at finding an adequate landing craft and artillery lighters.

As mentioned above, the first major landing exercise to take place in the interwar period occurred off of both Guantanamo Bay, Cuba, and Culebra, Puerto Rico, during the US Fleet's annual exercises. Accompanying the fleet was a portion of the Marine Corps Expeditionary Force, under the command of LtCol Richard M. Cutts, who were to test the possibilities of landing the 155mm (6.1in) gun and its accompanying 10-ton (10.1 tonne) tractor from ship to shore in small boats. Elements of the 9th Company, 10th Marine Regiment (Artillery) successfully landed one 155mm gun, two 75mm (2.95in) field guns, one 10-ton and two 5-ton tractors from the USS *Florida* off the US Naval Station at Guantanamo Bay, Cuba. During this exercise, 'close attention was paid to the training of the gun's crews and special details, the hardening of the men, and the testing of all material, and communication.' In March, the same company re-embarked for further tests held on the island of Culebra, Puerto Rico, where an additional force of Marines joined with the 9th Company and conducted a small advanced base exercise, with the force moving from ship to shore, controlled by the command element of the Control Force, US Atlantic Fleet. LtCol Cutts later remarked that 'it has been conclusively demonstrated that artillery up to and including 155mm guns and 10-ton tractors can be transported by battleships and landed in ship's boats.'

LtCol Cutts, however, cited the fact that the force landed under almost ideal conditions with a calm sea and moderate surf, something that 'will not always be the case', though he added that this did not make a landing 'impossible'. He nonetheless recommended that a lighter be developed to transport the heavy guns that could be 'grounded' on the beach and not self-propelled. In 1926, the first of such lighters were ready to be tested at the Norfolk Navy Yard with Cutts in attendance. In one of the first inklings of a change in the advanced base mission from a defensive to offensive nature, Major General Commandant John A. Lejeune dutifully reported in his annual report to the Secretary of the Navy for 1922 that 'while the exercises of 1922 were defensive in their nature, they brought out the difficulties of attack in landing operations against hostile opposition and the further presumption that the Marine Corps should be preparing for offensive landing operations in addition to the defensive advanced base work.'

A larger test for the MCEF came in the winter of 1924 during the Annual Fleet exercises off Panama and Culebra.

A separate Marine force under the command of Brigadier General Eli K. Cole, and designated the 'Black' force, had as its mission the 'seizure' of both the off-shore forts guarding the entrance to the Panama Canal, and once that mission had been accomplished, to sail to Culebra and dislodge the 'Blue' Marine Force, commanded by Colonel Dion Williams. The defences on Culebra, manned by a Marine advanced base force, complete with trench lines, armed with mortars and machine guns, barbed wire, anti-aircraft guns, and tanks positioned behind the defender's beach positions, awaited Cole's force of infantry from the 5th Marine Regiment, as well as Navy medical personnel and four US Army liaison officers who observed the exercise.

Landing on Culebra

After an initial landing on Culebra, the exercise umpires declared that the 'Black' force had failed to dislodge the defenders from their positions. This was not the only bad news for the proponents of an 'offensive-oriented' force. On board the Navy's transports, the attacking Marines had been lowered into the water and awaited the order to proceed to the shore five hours before the scheduled landing, with the result that many became seasick in the choppy waters. Also, as the landing craft headed to shore, many ended up on the wrong beaches or had become lost in the confusion. For its part, the post-exercise analysis faulted the Navy's inade-

quate naval gunfire support provided to the landing force. The one bright spot in the exercise was the fact that the 25-man Marine cargo outfit had successfully on-loaded and off-loaded supplies for the attacking force, a crucial success since, as Marines demonstrated later, combat loading, as it came to be called, was a critical element in the success of an amphibious landing.

The two notable features of the 1924 Winter Maneuvers on Culebra included the participation of an armoured whale-boat first used by the British at Gallipoli in 1915, called a 'beetle' boat, that could carry either a 75mm (2.95in) field gun or 100 riflemen. While the boat proved partially successful, the design had proven faulty, as well as it being extremely difficult to load and unload a field piece under actual combat conditions. The other landing vehicle tested was the 'Christie' amphibian tank, built by inventor and tank designer Walter Christie. Christie persuaded Marine Brigadier General Smedley D. Butler, and later MajGen John A. Lejeune, to allow the tank to accompany the fleet during the exercise, but the results were unimpressive. After being launched from a platform atop a submarine, the Christie

Below: The Marines continued to search for a suitable amphibian landing craft to bring troops ashore on an enemy-held beach. Here, the Christie landing vehicle, a forerunner of the Landing Vehicle Tracked (LVT), practices on Culebra.

tank, slow and taking on water, floundered in the surf and had to return to the mother ship. Landed separately from the exercise onto the shore, the Christie tank came ashore and impressed the leathernecks with its removable treads and manoeuvrability. Marine officers present at Culebra agreed that while the concept remained valid, the vehicle would require further refinements before more tests could be conducted with live troops. While the Marine Corps had expressed the desire that tests continue on the Christie amphibian tank, HQMC lacked the funds to pay for experimental models, and thus cancelled further Marine involvement in the project. Despite its obvious failure at Culebra, the Christie tank served as one of the earliest forerunners to the LVTs (Landing Vehicle Tracked) used by Marines during World War II.

Manoeuvres on Oahu

The last Marine advanced base exercise held during the 1920s prior to the deployments to China and Nicaragua in 1927 was held on the island of Oahu, Territory of Hawaii, during the Joint Army and Navy Exercises in the spring of 1925. As part of a combined force of sailors and soldiers, 1500 Marines of the 4th and 10th Marine Regiments acted as base seizure force and successfully overran the Army defenders dug in along the beaches near Fort Shafter and the Scholfield Army Barracks. Once again, however, the attacking Marines waited endlessly and uncomfortably in the small

ships' boats as the waves soaked them. When the order arrived to move to shore, the boats once again became lost, or proceeded ahead of the other waves out of order while others were too slow in reaching their designated line of departure to shore. From 1 to 4 May at Pearl Harbor, and later 1 to 5 June 1925, from the MCS at Quantico, VA, a post-exercise analysis headed by Col Robert H. Dunlap, who at the time was in charge of the Field Officers Course at the Marine Corps Schools, concluded once again that the Marine Corps needed 'to develop a boat suitable for landing the first waves ashore on a defended coast . . . . capable of being turned out in quantity once war is determined upon.' As an official Marine Corps history concluded, 'if there was one single unchanging thread in all of the fleet exercises during the 1920s, it was the constant recommendation that a suitable boat be developed to land the landing force.'

Despite the end of active Marine participation in the annual fleet exercises, due to expeditionary duty abroad (Nicaragua and China, respectively, in January and March 1927), as well as domestic duty at home guarding the US Mails from robberies, some Marines remained actively interested in testing boats and in writing doctrine, and some

Below: Marines land in practice assaults at the Marine Barracks, Quantico, VA, in the 1920s. The coxswains of the boats, like the Marines themselves, are extremely exposed to enemy fire, but boats like these were used up to the 1940s.

experimentation with landing lighters did take place. Nonetheless, active Marine participation in the annual exercises did not resume until 1932. In July 1926, a detachment of Marines under the command of Major Maurice E. Shearer reported to the US Navy Base at Hampton Roads, VA, where they tested two 50-foot motor lighters, one for landing troops and the other for landing artillery.

This continued interest in landing boats likewise led to a change in the curriculum at the Marine Corps Schools, particularly in the advanced Field Officers Course, where, due to the recommendations made by Dunlap's post-1925 exercise report, HQMC added forty-four hours to the five hours currently spent during the 1926–27 academic year in the syllabus in studying landing operations with the fleet during a naval campaign. Also additional to the MCS curriculum were subjects and lectures delivered by naval officers on such diverse topics as naval intelligence, strategy, naval history, and perhaps the most important subject of all, and one that would have a direct result on the success or failure of landing operations – naval gunfire support. By the early 1930s, the MCS at Quantico would become the 'center' of amphibious warfare studies. Another important event in 1927 was the recognition by the Joint Board of the Army and Navy of the pre-eminence of the Marine Corps in landing operations. To this end, the Joint Board assigned them the general function and responsibility to 'maintain forces for land operations in support of the fleet for the initial seizure of advanced bases and for such limited auxiliary land operations as are essential to the prosecution of a naval campaign.' The Joint Board further concluded that 'the Marines, because of the constant association with naval units will be given special training in the conduct of landing operations.' Despite the continued interest in the conduct of landing operations by the Marines, the deployment schedule and its subsequent drain on officers all but closed down the MCS from 1927 to 1929.

BIRTH OF THE FLEET MARINE FORCE AND THE TENTATIVE LANDING MANUAL 1931–1934

The withdrawal of Marines from Nicaragua and China that began in 1929 and continued through 1933 signalled a renewed effort on the part of HQMC to address the issue over the Marine Corps' role and mission as part of a naval campaign. Despite the Joint Board's recognition of the Marine

Above: Sailors and Marines tested a variety of landing craft during the interwar era. Here, two lighters sit side-by-side during trials to establish the best method of loading and unloading artillery, a key component in any landing force.

Corps' role as an advanced base force, a lack of manpower and a workable landing doctrine hampered headquarters in its efforts to create two forces, one for each coast and of equal strength, for advanced base duty with the respective fleets. This condition, in fact, lasted till 1933 when the last of the Marines permanently left Nicaragua.

By that time, however, the changes implemented in the MCS by MajGen Ben H. Fuller, who succeeded MajGen Wendell C. Neville as the Major General Commandant upon the latter's unexpected death in office in June 1930, began to take permanent hold in the curriculum which in turn provided the impetus to create a permanent advanced base force. With the terms of the Washington Naval Treaty now under severe criticism in US naval circles, due largely to Japan's aggression in Manchuria that began in 1931, and continued suspicions as to whether she had abided by the terms of that treaty, there was a slow movement toward a modest rearmament that picked up steam upon the election of Franklin D. Roosevelt as President of the United States in 1932.

MajGen Fuller, with the help of his assistant, BrigGen John H. Russell, struggled through the draconian budgets of the Herbert Hoover administration (1929–33), in order to keep the Marine Corps from being abolished or, as some critics of the Corps wanted, most notably Army Chief of Staff General Douglas MacArthur, absorbed into the US Army. Both Fuller and Russell set out to reinvigorate the Advanced Base Force with an entirely new force armed with an offensive base-seizing mission.

Despite the creation of the Fleet Marine Force in August 1933, and its permanent codification in December of that same year, the Marine Corps had not yet resolved its quest for a suitable landing craft. As early as April 1931, a board convened at Quantico where it conducted an exhaustive study to examine the use of 50-foot motor sailers in the landing of a 75mm (2.95in) howitzer and accompanying train and mount. While the board concluded that it was feasible to land this equipment ashore using the motor sailers, the body of opinion agreed that the 'ideal' surf conditions that existed during the experimental landing would not always be present and the tests needed to continue. The following year, in 1932, Marines conducted the first major exercise since 1925 off Oahu, Territory of Hawaii, and the results were not too encouraging.

Poor Results

During the 1932 Oahu Maneuvers, the 'Marines went ashore, waded through the surf, secured a beachhead and carried out all the details of the plan'. As Colonel Holland M. Smith, who later commanded the V Amphibious Corps during the Central Pacific Drive during World War II recalled, the results of this exercise, 'were not too encourag-

ing'. The Marines landed in standard Navy ships' boats, 'which were unsuitable for crossing reefs and riding the surf'. Also, the need for a retractable landing craft reappeared, as did the requirement of a sufficient number of boats that could carry the entire attacking force ashore in one assault. As Col Smith remembered: 'So small was the number of men we were able to land that the suppositional enemy would have wiped us out in a few minutes.' In short, Smith wrote: 'the Oahu operation revealed our total lack of equipment for such an undertaking, our inadequate training, and the lack of coordination between the assault forces and the simulated naval gunfire and air protection'. Smith concluded that 'I realized how badly prepared we were and how urgent was our need for further study and improvement of our methods. The doctrine of amphibious warfare was still in the theoretical stage.'

With the writing of the *Tentative Landing Manual* in 1934 Marines conducted several more exercises, though problems still persisted in such areas as landing craft, naval gunfire, and logistics. Both the Bureau of Construction and Repair (later in 1940 renamed Bureau of Ships or BuShips) and the Marine Corps' Equipment Board strove to develop suitable landing craft, though lack of funds and suitable

Marines were instructed to carry their weapons at 'high port' whenever hand-to-hand combat seemed likely.

The 'guard' position, used when faced with an enemy during hand-to-hand combat to keep him at bay.

Above: An early 'Higgins' Boat is ready to disembark a Marine truck in early 1940. The front-loading design underwent extensive trials and tests before it was adopted by the Marines, who went on to use it and its successors throughout the Pacific campaign.

designs hampered their efforts. General Merrill B. Twining, who as a young captain assisted in the revisions to the *Tentative Landing Manual* in the late 1930s, remarked that the Navy, due to both a lack of enthusiasm for amphibious warfare and funds, put the development of landing boats at the bottom of the list as the least important item on its rearmament agenda. Only through the efforts of a few energetic Navy officers in Construction and Repair and the persistence of Marines were suitable landing craft developed in time for the US entry into World War II.

The problems faced by the naval and Marine officers searching for suitable landing craft can be broken down into three distinct categories. These included (1) Landing Boats – in order to ferry troops from ship to shore; (2) Lighters – used to carry tanks and other vehicles; and (3) Amphibians – primarily used for fire support during an actual landing as an amphibious tank. In order to facilitate the design and development of landing craft for amphibious operations the Secretary of the Navy, in January 1937, convened a special board, comprised of the Chief of Naval Operations (CNO), the Major General Commandant of the Marines, and officials from the Bureaus of Construction and Repair and Ordnance.

The first problem tackled by this Landing Boats for Training Operations Board was to develop or find a suitable landing craft for landing operations. At the request of the Marine Corps, the Navy agreed to test a number of small boats that fitted the specifications of available deck space, handling facilities, and davit strength of the ships of 1935. Out of the nine boats offered for tests, the board selected five candidates, four fishing craft and one all-metal surf

boat, all of which proved unsatisfactory in all requirements after a lengthy period of evaluation, which took place off Hampton Roads, VA, near the Navy's major base at Norfolk.

After the failure to find a suitable 'off the shelf' candidate, the Bureau of Construction and Repair attempted to design and build their own landing craft, according to the specifications laid out by the Chief of Naval Operations that conformed to the present dimensions and capabilities of the ships designated to carry them. The 'Bureau Boat', as Marines and Navy officers called it, made its first appearance during the 1940 manoeuvres and again in 1941, and after much effort failed to meet the requirements of either service.

Another unexpected candidate came from a Louisiana shipbuilder and inventor named Andrew Jackson Higgins, who had placed a bid in 1935 with a boat he called the *Eureka*. While he declined to enter the bidding in 1935, Jackson wrote a letter to the Navy Department in October 1936 and offered his boat design to them, which he described as a 'troop carrying barge'. The *Eureka* boat was, as an official history stated, 'a boat of promising design'. Besides possessing a shallow draft and tunnel stern to protect the propeller when the boat retracted from the shore, it had a special bow which enabled it to run well up on low banks and beaches, and could retract easily from the beach back into the water.

Competition

Even as Higgins began to press the Navy Department with his design, some elements in the Navy, notably the Bureau of Construction and Repair, continued to push its 'Bureau Boat', based on the fact that it was more compatible than the *Eureka*. Furthermore, fleet officers complained that the *Eureka*'s 36-foot length was too long for the ship's davits. Nonetheless, once Marine officers saw what the *Eureka* landing craft could do, they wanted nothing else. This is not to say that the *Eureka* did not have problems – it did. During the manoeuvres held in the summer of 1941, Marine Sergeant MacGillivray, who was part of a 37mm (1.45in) anti-tank team with the 1st Marine Division, recalled one of the *Eureka*'s main drawbacks was its bulkheads, which were too high and necessitated considerable effort to scale over, which in turn exposed the occupants of the boat to enemy fire. MacGillivray remembered that 'I had difficulty in climbing down the sides of the boat which were extremely high, and once in the surf, oftentimes I would "disappear" as soon I stepped into the water because the gun barrel I carried was heavy and the boat bobbed up and down in the surf.' Higgins later resolved this problem by adding a ramp to the bow. The idea for a bow ramp ironically

Above: Marine tank crewmen of a M3 Stuart rest during a lull in the battle on Guadalcanal. The Stuart proved to be too light a tank for later actions, though it served as an effective infantry support vehicle in the jungle war in the Northern Solomons.

came from the Japanese, who had used a similar type of a landing craft while fighting the Chinese in September 1937 in Shanghai. Observed by then First Lieutenant Victor H. Krulak, who made a detailed report of the landing craft used by the Japanese, the bow ramp built into the *Eureka*, now renamed the Higgins' Boat, after its inventor, proved to be the deciding issue, as one of these boats successfully landed a small bulldozer during experiments conducted by HQMC. BrigGen Charles Barrett, one of the original authors of the *Tentative Landing Manual* and Maj Ernest E. Linsert reported to the Major General Commandant Thomas Holcomb that 'the Higgins Boats were quite acceptable'.

Insofar as tank lighters had been concerned, once again it was a matter of design, as both the Navy's Continuing Board and Bureau of Construction and Repair continued to press

for a tank lighter that could transport the Army's 15-ton (15.2 tonne) tank or Marine Corps' Marmon-Harrington tank. The Navy subsequently produced a 45-foot (13.7m) Bureau Boat that could carry one Army 15-ton tank (the M5 Stuart) or two Marine Marmon-Harrington tanks. When one lighter eventually sank with an Army tank on board during an exercise in the fall of 1940, the Navy once again turned to Higgins to design and build a suitable boat for the Marines and Army to use as a tank lighter.

Higgins versus the Bureau

During the summer of 1941, the Marines and the Navy tested the 45-foot Higgins design versus that of a 47-foot (14.3m) Bureau Boat. The results were predictable. The Higgins Boat proved, as Marine MajGen Holland M. Smith wrote, far superior to the 'heavy, slow, difficult to control, difficult to retract from the beach, and unpredictable power plants', on the Bureau Boats. When the US Army changed the requirement once again for the lighter to carry its heavier (30-ton (30.5-tonne)) M4 Sherman medium tank, Higgins redesigned his lighter to accommodate both the Army and Navy's requirements. In April 1942, impressed by the results of the Higgins design, President Roosevelt ordered that 500 of the now 50-foot (15.24m) Higgins-designed lighters be built by both the inventor and the Navy jointly.

The last boat developed that had a significant impact on the Marine Corps' development of its amphibious warfare doctrine had its origins in the 1924 exercises on Culebra. The Christie amphibian, while a failure, proved to be the genesis in the search for a vehicle that could take troops from ship to shore and bring them up and beyond the beachhead. The British had experimented with a similar design, and had created a rather successful tank that had amphibious capabilities – the Medium D – developed in the last few months of World War I. However, the British lost interest and instead concentrated on land tanks, and thus abandoned any further testing on what promised to be a revolutionary concept in armour design. Despite losing out in the development of an amphibious tank, the British Army retained its interest (and commitment) in the development of flotation devices for

tanks, which culminated in the invention of the DD tank flotation device used by the Allies during the landings at Normandy on 6 June 1944.

The US Marine Corps, which had developed a strong interest in tanks near the end of World War I, concluded as early as the 1920s that tanks could prove extremely effective not only in the defence of an advanced base, but in providing fire support to the assaulting troops. In 1923, the first Marine tank company had been organized, and a year later took part in the 1924 advanced base exercise on Culebra, acting as part of a mobile defence force. Along with the testing of the Christie amphibian (a failure from the operational viewpoint), the use of armour during a landing remained foremost in the minds of forward-thinking Marines, who saw tanks as a necessary part of any

Below: US Marines storm ashore from Higgins boats during an amphibious assault in the Southwest Pacific during World War II. Note the Browning machine gun mounted on the landing craft to provide local air defence or fire support.

Above: A Navy LCM ploughs through the surf to bring Marines and valuable cargo ashore during an amphibious landing. The boats like these used for landings were normally crewed by either Navy or Coast Guardsmen rather than Marines.

amphibious assault. Yet questions remained as to what type of tanks would be used, and what role they would play during an assault on an enemy beachhead. The *Tentative Landing Manual* of 1934 attempted to answer these two questions when the authors wrote that, 'the difficulties of transport and movement from ship to shore indicate that only light tanks can be used in the landing operation. These may be land tanks or amphibious tanks.' The concept of a landing vehicle capable of carrying troops and providing fire support had thus been born. Now Marines only needed a vehicle to carry out this mission.

The 'Alligator'

The landing vehicle that Marines had pressed for in order to successfully carry assault troops beyond the beachhead came not as a result of tests by either the Bureau of Construction and Repair or the Marine Corps' Equipment Board, but from a photograph in the 4 October 1937 edition of *Life Magazine,* which pictured a strange vehicle, called an 'Alligator' by its inventor Donald Roebling, that had been built to rescue victims trapped by hurricanes in Florida's often impassable Everglades. The 'Alligator', built

first with a steel and later an aluminum hull, weighed 14,350lb (6509kg) and was 24ft (7.3m) in length, and could travel up to 18mph (29km/h) on land and 2.3mph (3.7km/h) in water. Powered by a 92hp (68.6kW) Chrysler engine, it was propelled by a chain with built-in roller bearings, with a smooth steel channel around the track contour for the rollers to ride on while supporting the weight of the vehicle. The 'Alligator' went through several modifications before it came to the attention of the Marine Corps via Rear Admiral Edward C. Kalfbus, Commander, Battleships, Battle Force, US Fleet, to Marine MajGen Louis McCarthy Little who in turn showed it to MajGen Thomas Holcomb. Holcomb in turn passed it on to the Marine Corps' Equipment Board, which responded by sending one of its members, Maj John Kaluf, to Florida to meet Roebling. At Roebling's workshop in Clearwater, Maj Kaluf recalled that 'Roebling had a vehicle fully operational at the time and put it through every kind of test that I could dream up. . . .' Major Kaluf, taking about 400ft of 16mm film, reported back to the Equipment Board which recommended to MajGen Holcomb that the Marine Corps should 'procure a pilot model . . . for further tests under service conditions and during Fleet Exercise No 5'.

Both the Continuing Board and Bureau of Construction and Repair initially rejected Holcomb's request, citing lack of funds due to the development of suitable landing boats. The Major General Commandant persisted, however, and through supporters inside the Navy Department and in Congress obtained funds for Roebling to start work on what eventually became the basis for the Landing Vehicle Tracked (LVT) 1. By January 1940, the first model rolled out of the inventor's workshop with all of the changes including a further weight reduction to 7700lb (3492.6kg), and shortened in length to 20ft (6m) while its width was set at 8ft (2.4m). Its water speed was increased to between 8 to 10mph (12.9 to 16km/h). This model had greater buoyancy, loaded or empty, and was easier to steer. Roebling replaced the Chrysler engine with that of slightly faster Ford V8 95hp (70.8kW) Mercury engine. Further modifications included the addition of a 120hp (89.5kW) Lincoln-Zephyr engine requested by the Navy which enabled the vehicle to hit a maximum speed in water of 9.72mph (15.6km/h) and 29mph (46.7km/h) on land.

Field Tests

As for the 'Alligator's' field tests, the vehicle surpassed all expectations, as Marine, Navy, and Army officers observed the vehicle at the MCS at Quantico in October 1940. The major test for the 'Alligator' came during the Fleet Exercises Number 7, in January and February 1941 at Culebra, which turned out to be the last major exercise there before the US entered World War II in December 1941. During this exercise Captain Victor H. Krulak (later LtGen) along with Sergeant Clarence H. Raper and Corporal Walter L. Gibson, all members of the 1st Brigade staff, put the 'Alligator' through various tests. The vehicle lived up to all the expectations, with only two minor recommendations made by Marine officials to ensure acceptance by the Navy. The first centered on the material and construction of the vehicle. While the 'Alligator' was built primarily from aluminum (a relatively new material in this era) to increase its buoyancy, both Navy and Marine officers considered it not rugged enough for the work intended for the vehicle. The second problem centered on the vehicle's 'shoes' or cleats, that enabled it to plough through surf and onto the shore. These same officers believed that the vehicle's track would not endure the abrasive effect of sand and water. Other than these problems, the vehicle's performance was 'flawless', prompting the Navy to award Roebling a contract to redesign the vehicle to an all-steel configuration. With the assistance of Mr James M. Hait, Chief Engineer of the Food Machinery Corporation (FMC), located in nearby Dunedin and Lakeland, Florida, a group of design and engineering specialists totally redesigned the 'Alligator' to an all-steel, riveted vehicle. The Navy, pleased with the redesigned vehicle, awarded FMC a contract for an official design and further development of the 'Alligator' known officially as the LVT (1).

The Bureau of Ships likewise awarded FMC its first production contract for 200 more LVTs, with the first one coming off the assembly line in July 1941. By the end of World War II, over 15,654 LVTs of all types had been built, with FMC building over 11,251 of them while the Borg-Warner Corporation of Kalamazoo, MI, the Graham Paige Motors Corporation, and St Louis Car Company of St Louis, MO, built the additional 4403 vehicles.

In order to train Marines in the use of the LVT, HQMC established the Amphibian Tractor Detachment at Dunedin, FA, commanded by Maj William W. Davis. In time, the four

This Marine, of the 1st Marine Defense Battalion on Wake Island in December 1941, is wearing the typical attire of a US Marine during the early stages of the Pacific war. He is armed with a M1903 Springfield rifle, and wears the M1917 helmet with a light khaki uniform. He is carrying a gas respirator in the bag over his shoulder.

officers and thirty-three enlisted men, with Davis as their leader, became the nucleus for the training detachment from which, with the addition of other officers and men, was formed the 1st Amphibian Tractor Battalion. By 16 February 1942, the battalion comprised of four companies, including a headquarters and service company which had been merged with its parent unit, the 1st Marine Division, and saw its first action during the Guadalcanal campaign, where the LVTs performed yeoman service as cargo carriers, prior to their employment as assault vehicles during the landings in the Gilbert Islands on Tarawa in November 1943.

While Marines struggled to find suitable landing craft in order to transport assault troops ashore, they likewise dealt with doctrinal matters all of which had to be resolved before the amphibious assault became a reality. Building upon the success of the *Tentative Landing Manual*, Marine and Navy officers were assigned to the MCS to refine the doctrine further. The Marines concluded that the British landing at Gallipoli had failed not because of the 'combat' phase of the landing but due to a lack of follow-on pinpoint naval gunfire support, a poor command relationship between the naval task force commander and ground force commander, and the improper storage and unloading practices of critical supplies, known as 'combat loading'.

Naval Gunfire Support

One of the most important reasons the British landings at Gallipoli failed was over the lack of proper naval gunfire sup-

Above: A Marmon-Harrington Tank and LVT 1 rush past a Marine defensive position during manoeuvres at Onslow Beach, Marine Barracks, New River, NC (later known as Camp Lejeune, NC) during the Army–Marine manoeuvres of 1941.

port. British and French naval officers, adhering to the Nelsonian dictum that a 'ship is a fool to fight a fort', refused to bring their ships within the range of the Turkish guns to provide the ANZAC forces ashore with fire support, and thus negated any chance of the assault succeeding. Major Robert Dunlap wrote in a 1921 article in the *Marine Corps Gazette* that the main reason that Gallipoli failed was primarily due to the lack of suitable naval gunfire. In fact, during the 1920s, Marines understood that until naval officers realised that naval gunfire was critical to an amphibious landing, they could not even conceive of a successful landing taking place. Throughout the 1920s at the Marine Corps Schools, both Marine and naval officers struggled to arrive at a joint doctrine for naval gunfire, using Gallipoli as its example. The various fleet exercises of the 1920s pointed to the misunderstandings that existed within the Marine Corps' requirement for pre-landing naval bombardment.

A study completed at the Field Officer's Course at Quantico on naval gunfire at Gallipoli clearly stated that what little close-in fire support provided by naval vessels there was proved to be very effective in supporting the troops ashore. The study concluded that while the British naval commanders demurred in risking their ships within range of the beachhead, not one ship had been put out of action by the mobile Turkish artillery pieces, a fact often-times ignored in postwar analyses of Gallipoli. Dunlap concluded that the main reason the Gallipoli landing failed had been due to the fact that the assault waves went ashore unprotected, and thus the troops were pinned down on the beaches where the Turkish guns then proceeded to decimate them. The study's conclusion was simple: 'whatever Naval artillery support is decided upon, some of it should closely accompany the attacking troops.'

Difficulties

When the Marine Corps began to write the *Tentative Landing Manual*, the Navy assigned to it one of its officers, Lt Walter C. Ansel, who in time became one of the strongest and most strident advocates of the necessity of naval gunfire support during a landing operation. Stressing the importance of Ansel's appointment to the board, Major General Commandant Ben H. Fuller commented that 'he doubtless will be in a position to obtain informally naval thought on questions of naval doctrine which may arise.' In fact, one of the first problems examined by the *Tentative Landing Manual* was naval gunfire support. While the authors of the manual stressed the similarities of naval gunfire with that of conventional land artillery, they concluded that the presence of troops in the water heading for shore complicated proper fire support. The manual laid out the principles of fire direction, the nature of the projectiles, magazine capacity, and muzzle velocities and trajectories of weapons, and in the end the authors of this landmark publication had laid out a sound, though untested, doctrine for naval gunfire.

While the landing manual established the basic principles for naval gunfire support, there still existed problems in the types of projectiles the Navy planned to use, and the range that naval gunfire support ships would provide for the assault force. While Marine planners concluded that one possibility to overcome these problems included the use of aircraft, it was no substitute for the possibility that weather and other factors might inhibit proper close-in air support during a landing. Also, another problem considered, though neglected at the time of the writing of the chapter on naval gunfire, was the type of ammunition to be used. The high-powered naval guns with their flat trajectory and specialized armour-piercing shells, while excellent for fighting another ship, proved to be inadequate in knocking out reinforced bunkers,

such as those the Japanese forces employed at Tarawa in November 1943, with the result that the bunker remained intact and able to spray the landing area with deadly machine gun and artillery fire. As the landing on Tarawa demonstrated, in fact, while armour-piercing shells proved effective at smashing some masonry and lightly reinforced bunkers, they could not take out the most heavily-fortified land targets. Instead, the US Navy discovered that bombardment ammunition, with its surface-burst ammunition (in effect, sending up thousands of fragmentary pieces) was better suited against scattered emplacements and enemy personnel.

Specific Fire Missions

Nonetheless, the men dealing with naval gunfire support considered the three types best adapted to perform specific fire missions – close support, deep support, counterbattery, and interdiction missions – as well as the type of personnel to be used to call in such fire missions ashore. Here, the committee recommended three classes of personnel to be used in calling for naval gunfire: aerial observers; shipboard; and once the landing force had landed, shore fire control parties. While Lt Ansel at first recommended trained naval officers to be used in such a capacity, it was not until 1941

Below: An early LVT 1, seen here on Guadalcanal. During the campaign on this island, the LVTs served effectively as cargo carriers, supplying the Marines in the field across the rugged, almost impassable jungle terrain.

that Marines discovered that its own artillery officers made excellent onshore spotters, since they could not only relay the type target and ammunition to be used, but could better pinpoint the accuracy of the naval gunfire. Here, a trained Marine artillery officer and radio crew team formed into a specialized unit later known as ANGLICO (Air Naval Gunfire Liaison Company) with a naval officer serving as an assistant. In time, ANGLICO teams became indispensable in directing precise, accurate naval gunfire during an amphibious assault against land targets during World War II in both the Pacific and in Europe.

COMMAND RELATIONSHIPS

Besides naval gunfire, one of the most difficult problems that the *Tentative Landing Manual* attempted to resolve was over the proper command relationship between the commander, naval task force and commander, ground forces.

From the time of the earliest advanced base exercises beginning in 1903 up through 1943, this remained a constant irritant between the Navy and Marines over 'who had control of the landing force' during particular intervals of a landing. While the *Tentative Landing Manual* attempted to resolve this issue by stating that the attack force commander was 'to be the senior naval officer of the fleet units making up the attacking force, and in charge of all the forces necessary to conduct a landing operation', it nonetheless failed to resolve a lingering difficulty as to when the ground force commander assumed tactical control of the forces ashore. Here, the *Tentative Landing Manual* was extremely vague, since it placed the 'commander of the landing force under

Below: One of the most important aspects of a successful landing operation was proper naval gunfire support. Here, 5in (127mm) naval guns fire a supporting barrage as Marines proceed towards the shore in LVTs.

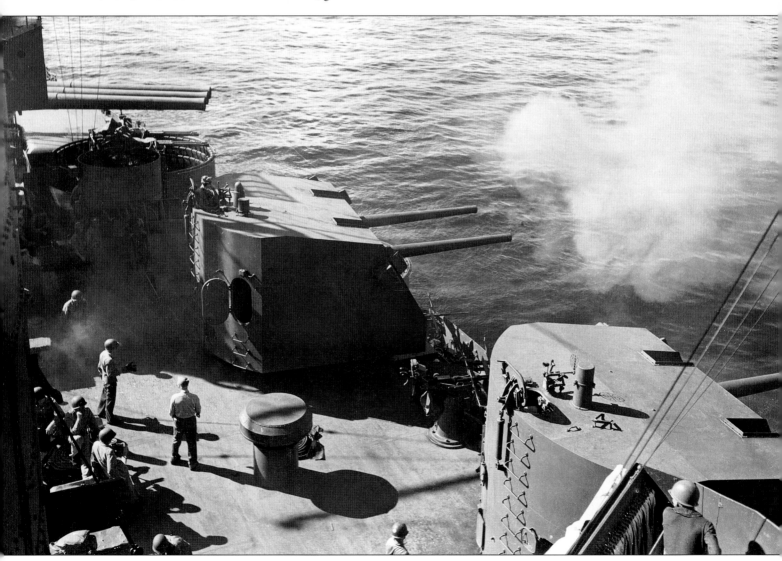

Above: Once ashore, Marines sought to push inland very fast in order to prepare the way for the follow-on forces. Here the difficulties of co-ordinating the movement of men and material on a crowded beach are graphically illustrated.

the command of the attack force commander throughout the operation'. This settled nothing, and pleased no one, since it gave the naval commander total control of the land forces ashore, a point sure to be contested since it meant interference from someone believed to be unfamiliar with land warfare. This is precisely what occurred during the landing on Guadalcanal, when Admiral Richmond Kelley Turner, Commander of the Amphibious Task Force, sought to exercise his command authority over MajGen Alexander A. Vandegrift's 1st Marine Division when it went ashore on 7 August 1942. This brought nothing but confusion, which eventually necessitated a conference on the island of Noumea between Fleet Admiral Chester Nimitz and the Commandant of the Marine Corps Thomas Holcomb in early 1943. The tentative compromise reached there has remained in effect ever since, and has proved to 'smooth over' what was a contentious issue between the Navy and Marines.

This solution agreed upon by the Navy and Marines on Noumea in effect gave the Commander, Amphibious Task Force (CATF) control over all forces while afloat. Once the amphibious force had landed, command then transferred to the Commander, Landing Force (CLF), who controlled the ground forces ashore. While some problems still developed between the respective Navy and Marine commanders, the agreement that established the relationship between the CATF and CLF was a milestone in the development of US amphibious warfare.

COMBAT LOADING/OFF-LOADING AND LOGISTICS

Gen Alfred H. Noble recalled that, in the writing of the *Tentative Landing Manual,* no other problem proved as difficult as logistics and the development of proper combat loading and off-loading procedures. As a student at the Field Officers' Course (1929–1932) the general recalled one of the instructors, Maj Charles Barrett, who stood up before a group of officers and said, 'If Gallipoli has proved anything it's proven that landing operations, even against opposition is comparatively simple. It has also proven that keeping troops ashore and keeping them fighting is even more difficult than the landing.' Gen Noble, in fact, admitted that up to 1929, nobody had considered logistics as a major concern during a landing operation, yet in the long run it proved to be the key to the success or failure.

Insofar as logistics had been concerned, the *Tentative Landing Manual* emphasized the overriding importance of prioritizing the needs of the landing force when loading and off-loading an amphibious transport. Whereas at Gallipoli and in the advanced base exercises critical equipment and ammunition had been placed at the bottom of the hold of the ship with no thought given to its importance in the period immediately after the landing, the authors of the

Tentative Landing Manual emphasized that, besides proper loading techniques, equipment and supplies which would be required immediately to sustain the landing needed to be loaded last. Also, the Marine officers assigned to write this portion of the manual standardized the procedures for both embarkation and disembarkation of logistical support. These procedures included preparation of embarkation forms, loading plans, and set forth the techniques to be used in the proper combat loading of assault ships.

Teething Problems

While Marine planners wrestled with the establishment of proper embarkation and disembarkation of critical supplies, it would, in fact, take the landings on Guadalcanal and later Tarawa to work out the 'bugs' in the system, particularly in the prioritizing of supplies to be off-loaded in the immediate period of the landing. As discovered on Guadalcanal, besides the fact that the Navy evacuated the area before an impending Japanese naval task force heading toward the island, and before it could unload all the supplies that the Marines required to sustain themselves ashore, the storage and off-loading techniques had either damaged or misplaced critical logistical support such as ammunition and food. Likewise on Tarawa, it was realized that the most critical needs of the landing force – water, ammunition, and medical supplies – had been placed on ships that had yet to be unloaded, while other less critical supplies were readily available to the landing force. While planners could theorize on the requirements of a landing force, it would take an actual landing under combat conditions to establish sound embarkation and disembarkation procedures.

One last point on the requirements of proper loading/off-loading procedures centered around tactical organizations. One of the few successes of the 1924 Culebra Maneuvers was the 25-man team put together by Col Dion Williams to off-load cargo during the exercise. Building on that success, the authors of the *Tentative Landing Manual* created a beach party headed by a beachmaster, 'a special task organization, commanded by the commander, landing force.'

The Beachmaster

The beachmaster was in overall command of the beach area, and had the primary responsibility of keeping the beach uncongested in order that logistics and follow-on forces could move ashore unhindered. The beach party had primarily naval functions such as naval reconnaissance and marking of the beaches, markings of hazards to navigation, control of boats, evacuation of wounded, and in the unloading of logistics. Its composition came from either the landing force, medical, engineers, work details from the rifle battalions, military police, communications, and chemical warfare personnel. As events turned out later on Guadalcanal, this proved totally unsatisfactory, as infantrymen, who would rather have faced the Japanese, had been chosen to fill the unwelcome role as stevedores, unloading the navy transports. Many of them simply lumped all supplies together, unmarked and on top of each other, causing vital material to become either damaged or lost. HQMC attempted to resolve this prior to the Guadalcanal landing in July 1942 with the issuance of a standard operating procedure designed to establish clear guidelines for the off-loading of supplies. This problem was later resolved with the creation of a Shore Party, later known as Force Troop, in mid-1943 as Fleet Marine Force Pacific (FMFPac) absorbed the lessons of the fighting on Guadalcanal.

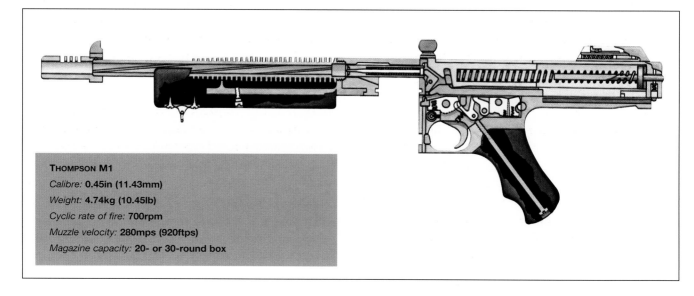

THOMPSON M1
Calibre: **0.45in (11.43mm)**
Weight: **4.74kg (10.45lb)**
Cyclic rate of fire: **700rpm**
Muzzle velocity: **280mps (920ftps)**
Magazine capacity: **20- or 30-round box**

In short, the Marines made great strides toward the establishment of a sound amphibious warfare doctrine and set of procedures, though it took the landing on Tarawa to validate and test the validity of the principles of the *Tentative Landing Manual*. Despite the setbacks of the manoeuvres held during the 1920s, particularly the 1924 and 1925 winter manoeuvres off Culebra and Oahu respectively, Marines continued to study and experiment with proper landing procedures. Despite expeditionary duty to China and Nicaragua in the late 1920s Marine officers incorporated many of the lessons learned in these exercises into the curriculum of the Marine Corps Schools in advance of better times ahead when they could devote their full energies to the codification of a sound landing doctrine.

Some of the lessons learned during these exercises were the requirements for better landing craft and procedures regarding naval gunfire, as well as combat loading/off-loading procedures. When Marines sat down to begin writing the basic tenets of the *Tentative Landing Manual* in 1931, these problems were, in fact, the first ones resolved, though it would take the test of war to correct the deficiencies, and there were many that existed in these guidelines. Nonetheless, the authors of the *Tentative Landing Manual* realized from the start that the British failure at Gallipoli could be over-

come, though it would take another decade and a half of hard, thoughtful work to resolve those problems of a doctrine that required sound procedures from everything that included embarkation and disembarkation, naval gunfire support, well-defined command relationships, and well-trained assault troops. Without any one of these, the success of a landing operation could be placed in jeopardy.

Need for Manpower

While the Marine Corps encountered doctrinal problems of untested procedures and practices insofar as logistics, naval gunnery, and command relationships were concerned, as well as the lack of suitable landing boats and lighters for artillery and tanks, manpower remained a critical component of any landing doctrine. With this in mind, HQMC centered the bulk of its efforts during the interwar period up until World War II on the recruiting and training of Marines in order to execute the landing doctrine developed during the 1920s and 1930s.

CHAPTER 3

Marine Corps Recruitment and Training 1919–1945

In the aftermath of World War I, Marine numbers dropped dramatically, and recruiters fought both to keep the Corps up to strength and to ensure a high quality of recruit. New training programmes reflected the hard lessons learned in the war, and by the time of Pearl Harbor, the Marines were ready for battle.

APART FROM THE organizational, doctrinal, and technical aspects that prepared Marines for combat, both recruitment and training played a significant part in the development of the Marine Corps' ability to carry out amphibious assaults from Guadalcanal to Okinawa. This was a process that began, in fact, during the interwar period (1919–1941), and had at its core the system established by the US Marine Corps prior to the United States' entrance into World War I. Upon demobilization in 1919, HQMC made a concerted effort not only to recruit qualified and motivated manpower, but to train this force properly and efficiently as a cohesive combat organization. In fact, the training programme instituted by HQMC in the aftermath of World War I retained many of the features that had been introduced as early as 1911 by Major General Commandant William P. Biddle. This included a systematic and uniform three-month period of recruit training at either of the three (later two) recruit depots, and effective branch and unit training that in time became centered on the lessons of World War I, insofar as small unit and individual training was concerned.

World War I saw recruiters introduce many novel methods of inducement in order to attract volunteers into the Marine Corps. These included appeals to manhood, patriotism, travel, and sense of adventure. During the interwar era the HQMC retained the US Marine Corps' first recruitment department, which included the Publicity Bureau, an office that was designed to keep the US Marine Corps and its activities in the forefront of the American public's consciousness. The Marine Corps' splendid combat record during World War I, and the acquired slogans of 'Devil Dogs' (given to the Marines by a respectful German adversary), 'First to Fight', and 'Tell that to the Marines', (which had its origins with the British Royal Marines) gave an initial boost to postwar recruitment. Despite austere budgets, manpower ceilings, and few enlistees, the Marine Corps continued to attract a sufficient number of men looking for adventure and travel, or hoping to learn a skill or, as was the case after the onset of the Great Depression (1929–1940), as a means of steady employment. With this small cadre of military professionals recruited and trained during the interwar era, the Marine Corps laid the foundation of its amphibious assault force, starting as the Marines returned from France in 1919 up until the eve of the United States' entrance into World War II.

RECRUITMENT AND TRAINING OF 'A FORCE IN READINESS'

During World War I, the US Marine Corps recruited an estimated 57,144 men, with a small percentage of this figure

Left: A Marine crouches, ready to fire on a suspected enemy position, in the jungles of the Northern Solomons in 1943–44. The density of the jungle made the fighting a very personal experience for anyone involved.

being conscripts by the time of the Armistice on 11 November 1918. Upon demobilization, the US Marine Corps reverted back to its authorized strength of 27,400 officers and enlisted men, though through attrition the force dwindled rapidly to around 20,000, far below its authorized strength, fixed by Congress as always at one-fifth of the overall strength of the US Navy. On 4 December 1918, voluntary enlistments, curtailed due to the war, resumed in the US Marine Corps, and proved to be slow with the wartime emergency over. In fact, during the immediate postwar period, HQMC, in order to attract young men to its ranks, enlisted men in the Corps for two, three and four years. In order to attract mature young men to the Marines, both Major Generals Barnett and later Lejeune urged the recruitment of former soldiers and sailors in order to cut down on the number of desertions quite common during peacetime. Upon the cessation of hostilities HQMC discontinued many wartime measures, such as the recruitment of women ('Marinettes'), who served in primarily clerical positions at headquarters and at the Marine Corps' Supply Depot located in Philadelphia, PA. Many of these same women stayed on as civilian employees at HQMC after the war, and

Below: A US Marine Recruiting Office in the 1920s. The end of World War I saw a reduction in every participant's armed forces, and the Marines were no exception. To counter this loss of men they pursued an active recruitment policy.

proved to be of immense value, setting the precedent for the permanent recruitment of women during World War II.

Recruitment and Enlisted Recruit Training 1920–1936

While manpower figures for 1919 through 1921 stabilized, both officer and enlisted recruitment suffered, due largely to the economic boom that attracted many potential recruits away from the Marine Corps (and other services) during the period immediately after World War I. While both Major Generals Barnett and Lejeune attempted a variety of measures that included increased pay and shorter enlistments, recruiters nonetheless had a difficult time in meeting their assigned quotas. As a result, the manpower levels in the Marine Corps dipped below 19,000.

In order to stimulate recruiting during the era, HQMC turned to its Publicity Bureau, based in New York City, in order to keep the general public aware of past exploits in World War I and of its present day activities. In addition to this emphasis on publicity, HQMC, in order to meet the shortfall in manpower in 1920 and 1921, relied upon both traditional methods of inducements as well as some not so traditional methods in their efforts to raise manpower for service with the Marines. Sergeant William A. Bihary, who had served in Haiti, Dominican Republic (1915–1917), and in all of the major battles in France including Belleau Wood during World War I, recalled that shortly after returning home from occupation duty in Germany, he had received a letter from HQMC encouraging him to re-enlist for another tour of duty. Sergeant Bihary looked at the letter and said, 'four years were enough for me!' Another method included the transfer of men from the Marine Corps Reserve over to the Regular Marine Corps, a practice carried out for only a short period of time, and eventually dropped as the wartime emergency ended and enlistments in the Marine Corps became voluntary once again.

In fact, both Major Generals Barnett and Lejeune spent the bulk of their time as Commandant attempting to recruit a suitable number of men for the Marine Corps. The manpower situation became so critical that at one point during Lejeune's commandancy separations and discharges exceeded enlistments. In order to stimulate recruiting, HQMC instituted several programs designed to encourage young men to enlist. Besides the usual promises of pay, adventure and travel, the

Above: Future US Marines stand at attention at Yemassee, SC, on their way to Marine Corps Recruit Depot at Parris Island, SC. Although recruit numbers were down after World War I, the Marine Corps remained selective in its intake.

Marine Corps began to emphasize education as a part of its recruiting program. The first of these educational benefits to be offered was through the Marine Corps Institute, founded in 1919. Established with the cooperation of the Scranton School of International Correspondence, both Major General John A. Lejeune and Brigadier General Smedley D. Butler organized the Marine Corps Institute in order to promote education in the ranks of the Marines. Here, Marines could take a correspondence course that ranged from mechanics to accounting and complete the course while deployed or in garrison. Upon the completion of the course, the Marine took a proctored examination and, having successfully completed the course, received a certificate that the leatherneck could show to a prospective employer or use to receive college credit.

The second solution to the recruiting problem was to broaden the recruiting campaign. Here, HQMC created what were known as 'Roving Marines'. Made up of Marines who had seen active service and selected from the various posts, ships, and stations where Marines were serving, these 'Roving Marines' performed vaudeville performances to show the positive benefits of joining the Marines. As Major General Lejeune wrote in his annual report for 1920, the purpose of the 'Roving Marines' was 'to show the country the sort of men that the Marine Corps makes out of the youngsters who enlist as well as to advertise the service for

the purpose of getting recruits'. The 'Roving Marines' appeared in over 202 towns and cities across the United States and attracted an estimated 1,000,000 people to their performances. As for the effectiveness of these travelling spokesmen for the Marine Corps, Major General Lejeune stated that beginning in April to June 1920, the end of the fiscal year, 'enlistments exceeded separations from the service', with the net gain readily apparent. One last method of recruitment was the placement of articles and advertisements about the Marine Corps by the Publicity Bureau. Because the Marine Recruiting Service was small at this time, prospective Marines were either to submit a request by mail or fill out the form attached to the article. Upon receipt of this letter or filled-in form, a Marine recruiter made a contact, and after screening a prospective recruit, had the individual take a physical by an approved physician, and if qualified, report for processing and shipment to one of the two recruit depots where the process to make them Marines commenced.

Whatever the situation, Major General Commandant Lejeune and his successors demanded from the officers and men assigned to recruiting duty a high quality of young applicants to the Marine Corps. To ensure a reduction in the desertion and disciplinary rates, HQMC raised the age of an enlistee to 21 years while an 18 year-old could enlist with one or more parent or guardian's consent. As Lejeune emphasized in his annual report for 1920: 'The combined effect of constantly hammering at the recruiting service, the advantages we really have to offer, and the gradual lessening of the demand for labor in industrial life are now beginning to have a very noticeable effect.' In short, the main task of

Marine recruiters during the 1920s and early 1930s was to 'gain contact with great numbers of these young men, find out what qualifications they possess and select for enlistment those who have the necessary qualifications – mental, moral, and physical – to perform well the varied and important duties of a Marine.' As time wore on, the search for qualified recruits became increasingly difficult, though HQMC persisted in its efforts.

Typical Recruits

As for the young men whom the US Marine Corps attracted into its ranks, the vast majority of them came either from the streets of the major cities, or from the many farm communities where the postwar boom came to a sudden end with the Armistice. One such Marine, Private Russell F. Colbert, typified the type of young man entering the Marine Corps during the 1920s. After having served aboard a tramp oil steamer as a merchant seaman, Colbert decided to enlist in the Marine Corps in order to learn a trade as an electrician. After enlisting in Columbia, SC, he boarded a train bound for Yemassee, SC, and from there to Port Royal (Beaufort, SC), where the prospective recruits were then transported across Port Royal Sound in a Navy steamer to the Marine Corps Recruit Depot, Parris Island. Pulling into the marina near the Lyceum, the recruits looked up to see standing above them a rather gruff-looking gunnery sergeant, who barked at the Navy coxswain, 'Get them the hell out'ta here, Take'em back to where the hell you got'em.' Colbert recalled that, after a momentary pause, the sergeant 'relented', and told the sailor, 'Okay, you might as well bring'em up here, and I'll try and make something of them.'

After receiving the customary greetings, the sergeant then marched the recruits over to the mess hall and fed them. They were then marched over to the post infirmary, where the recruits were given haircuts, a battery of shots, and issued a blue denim fatigue uniform that caused one Marine veteran of the era to recall that it resembled those given to prisoners in the state penitentiary: leggings, a campaign hat, boondocker shoes, underwear, a straight razor, soap, a steel metal bucket, and a scrub brush. Formed into a four-platoon company of seventy men each, the recruits then met their drill instructors who took charge of their recruits and began the process of making Marines out of civilians. Treating the recruits fairly though with firmness, the drill instructors, marksmanship coaches, and range instructors had only one goal: to make good Marines.

Parry left: a move taught to recruits which was designed to ward off an attack from the left by an enemy bayonet.

Parry right: without changing hands or grip, the recruit could equally well defend himself against an attack from the right.

Recruit training during the interwar period at either of the two recruit depots (Parris Island, SC, and San Diego, CA) lasted anywhere from seven to ten weeks, normally built around a 77-day training cycle. The first three weeks consisted of an introduction to naval and military courtesy, health and hygiene, military discipline, physical fitness training, and endless hours of close order drill. Here the recruits were broken down and stripped of their civilian identity, to be replaced by one that was completely Marine. The next, or second, phase of a recruit's introduction to military life in the Marine Corps was rifle marksmanship, the single most important part of a Marine recruit's training. Here their training lasted nearly three weeks, broken down into 'grass week', or 'snapping in', where the recruit received instruction from qualified range instructors on proper shooting techniques and positions, target identification, weapons nomenclature of the 1903 Springfield bolt-action rifle, and 'dry' firing. The second week of marksmanship training was practice firing, with the last being devoted to qualification week. It was here that Marines qualified as experts, sharpshooters, and marksmen. As an added incentive, all Marines who qualified with the service rifle were given an additional five to ten dollars a month in their pay. It must be stressed that above all else, the Marines placed as great an emphasis on marksmanship during recruit training then as they do today. The record of Marine sharpshooters at Belleau Wood in June 1918 serves as testimony to the standards that were acheived.

Above: Marine recruits train at Parris Island, SC, during the interwar era. Climbing ropes not only improved recruits' fitness levels – as Marines they would be expected to climb down into a ship's boats before conducting an amphibious landing.

Last Phase of Training

The last phase of recruit training consisted of inspections, close order drill, basic infantry skills, and weapons familiarization with grenades, the Browning Automatic Rifle (BAR), gas and chemical training, and the .45in (11.43mm) calibre pistol. Marines likewise received training in use of the bayonet and lessons in first aid. While Marine officials placed emphasis on teaching basic infantry skills, they normally left it to the Marine's unit, once he reported in from recruit training, to teach the new Marine skills such as patrolling and scouting.

After graduating from recruit training, Marines such as Private Colbert were either shipped directly to join a Marine unit on expeditionary duty in Nicaragua or China, or were sent to an Army or Navy technical school. At the various posts and duty stations Marines received further instruction in weapons familiarization, basic infantry tactics, and drill and ceremonies. In Nicaragua after 1928, brigade headquarters established what later – during the Vietnam War – became known as 'Division Schools', whereby Marines who had served in the field fighting guerrillas taught the recently-arrived Marines enemy tactics, patrolling, scouting, familiarization with Marine heavy and

Above: Bayonet training was one of the most important aspects in Marine recruit training during the interwar era. Here, Marine recruits under instruction practice bayonet thrusts. All recruits underwent training in basic infantry skills.

light weapons, use of the machine gun, Stokes mortars, and grenades. Marine officers received similar, though more intense, training.

Recruitment and enlisted recruit training changed very little between 1920 and 1936. While recruiting levels during the 1920s were never really good, Marine recruiters nonetheless worked hard at enlisting qualified young men into the ranks of the Marine Corps, and in the end their persistence paid large dividends with the high quality of men accepted into the ranks of the Corps. One noticeable effect on HQMC's desire for a quality recruit was a drop in the overall desertion and disciplinary rates. As the postwar economic boom ended, and with the onset of the Great Depression that saw unemployment soar, the Marine Corps filled its ranks with many of the young men that would become platoon sergeants and senior staff noncommissioned officers during World War II, and who would perform magnificently in combat as a part of the 'Old Breed' on such battlefields as Guadalcanal, Tarawa, Iwo Jima and Okinawa.

As for training, despite the austere budget, manpower shortages, and expeditionary duty in Nicaragua and China, recruit and individual training in the Marine Corps changed very little. While problems did occur among young Marines in the handling of weapons such as BARs, machine guns, and grenades in Nicaragua, they nonetheless performed superbly in combat against the *sandinistas,* and on peace enforcing

duty in China during the 1920s and early 1930s. When problems did appear, HQMC established special schools such as the briefly-organized Sergeants Course at Quantico in 1923, and brigade schools in Haiti, the Dominican Republic, and Nicaragua, in order to teach to new arrivals basic Marine infantry skills, that included patrolling, scouting, and weapons employment and handling. In 1929 and 1930, HQMC established special Infantry Weapons Schools at the Marine Barracks at San Diego and Quantico in order to correct some of deficiencies in performance discovered in combat in Nicaragua. Here, Marine non-commissioned officers and company-grade officers received in-depth instruction in weapons maintenance, handling, and tactical deployment. Despite the lack of funds and manpower, the Marine Corps during this era could still proudly state: 'We still make'em like we used to.'

Officer Enlistment and Training, 1919–1936

Prior to World War I, Marine officers normally came directly from the United States Naval Academy at Annapolis, from military academies such as the Virginia Military Institute in Lexington, VA, and the Citadel, in Charleston, SC, direct appointments from civilian life, and from the ranks of enlisted men. During the war, officers were in such great demand that besides the normal sources for Marine Corps officers, Marine recruiters sought qualified officer applicants at US universities and colleges, though, after October 1917, the main source of new officers came from the ranks. Commenting on the latter source of officers, Major General George Barnett wrote in his annual report for 1918: 'This policy has been strictly carried out, and, in my opinion, the results shown have fully justified the adoption of such a system.' Commanding officers, attached to the Marine Brigade in France and units elsewhere, identified applicants for commissions as second lieutenants from the enlisted ranks, who were then given proficiency and intelligence tests and, if found qualified, reported for further training at Quantico, VA. Here they underwent an intensive officer's training that normally lasted three months, studying such subjects as infantry drill or the 'School of the Soldier', chemical warfare, platoon and company tactics, weapons maintenance, and naval law and customs. After successfully completing this rigorous training, these young second lieutenants soon found themselves either in France or serving with Marines in Hispaniola. Nonetheless, as a result of the fighting and the need for additional company-grade officers due to the casualty rates, Barnett's policy of commissioning qualified NCOs proved well founded. Three of the many Marine officers that later reached the general officer ranks this way during World War I were Sergeants Gerald C. Thomas and Merwin H. Silverthorn, and Lewis B. 'Chesty' Puller. All distinguished themselves in combat, and established a precedent that the Marine Corps would follow as it mobilized for World War II.

Officer Retention

At the war's conclusion, the main question for the Marine Corps revolved around officer retention and professional education and development. In order to resolve the first issue of retention, at the end of the war Major General George Barnett convened the first of two specially appointed boards to deal with this issue, and the status of those officers such as Lieutenant Thomas who had served honorably and competently in combat, but due to demobilization and a cutback in officer strength would either be forced out of the Marine Corps entirely or revert back to their enlisted rank. The first board, headed by Major John H. Russell, a Naval Academy graduate, favoured the retention of only those officers either commissioned before the war or who had graduated from the Naval Academy or some other prestigious institution as well as having some refinements as 'gentlemen'. Even while the Russell Board met, a cabal to remove Major General Commandant Barnett from office, engineered by Colonel Smedley D. Butler and his powerful congressman father, Thomas S. Butler, succeeded in bringing disrepute on the eventual findings of the Russell Board, which both men agreed did little to reward those Marine officers who had demonstrated proven ability in France or on expeditionary duty, and went too far in elevating men whom the Butlers believed were 'swivel chair warriors', or those that had

remained at headquarters during the war. In order to resolve the controversy MajGen Barnett's successor, MajGen John A. Lejeune, immediately reconvened another board, headed by his friend and fellow Fourth Brigade colleague, Brigadier General Wendell C. 'Whispering Buck' Neville, whose findings came to the opposite conclusion, and placed greater emphasis on retaining the younger company grade officers such as Jerry Thomas and Melvin W. Silverthorn, since it was through such men that MajGen Lejeune had hoped to revitalize an officer corps which he believed had become stagnant. In the end HQMC compromised and retained an equal number from each board, which seemed for the time being to quell the controversy.

Major General Lejeune's goal of revitalizing the Marine Corps' officer corps and its advanced base mission centered upon the abolition of the antiquated practice of promotion by seniority, to be replaced by that of selection and merit. Despite his best efforts, this was one part of the Major General Commandant's program that failed to make it through Congress, due largely to the efforts of those who favoured the old system both in the Marine Corps and in the Senate. Eventually, under Major General Commandant John H. Russell in 1935, the Marine Corps adopted promotion by selection and merit, despite the storm of protest from almost over half of the Corps' field grade officers. Nonetheless, Lejeune's other programmes, focused around officer and enlisted education, succeeded with the opening

Below: The most important training for any Marine was rifle marksmanship. Here, Marines practice firing the M1 Garand rifle during the early years of World War II. Note that these recruits wear the pith helmets with a Marine Corps emblem.

Above: Marine officer candidates train on the obstacle course at Marine Corps Barracks, Quantico, VA, during World War II. As might be expected, officer training was more thorough and longer-lasting than that for enlisted men.

up of The Basic School, for newly-commissioned second lieutenants, The Marine Corps Infantry Officers' School, The Company Officers' School, and a Field Officers' School at Quantico, which soon became the hub of the Marine Corps' professional military education system. By the end of the decade, and despite the deployments to China and Nicaragua, as well as domestic duties in the 1920s, the Marine Corps had established an excellent, if only basic, school system for its newly-commissioned second lieutenants, company grade, and field grade officers at Quantico. Marine officers likewise attended both the US Army School of the Line, and Command and General Staff College at Fort Leavenworth, KS, and the Army Infantry Officer's Course at Fort Benning, GA, as well as the higher echelon schools located at the Army and Navy War Colleges.

At the Marine Corps Schools at Quantico, particularly in reference to the Infantry Officers' School and Company Officers' School, Marine officials placed great emphasis upon the US Army's Infantry Drill Regulations (IDRs) and its Field Service Regulations (FSRs), especially the 1923 edition, since they reinforced the lessons learned by the Marines and Army in the American Expeditionary Force in World War I, particularly in regard to combined arms war-

fare and infantry combat. Marine officers also attended the Army's School of the Line and Infantry Officers' Course at Fort Benning, GA, and the Command and Staff College, at Fort Leavenworth, KS, where Army instructors further imparted the lessons of the fighting on the Western Front to Marine officers.

Course Curricula

For Marine field grade officers, the curriculum likewise reflected the lessons of the fighting in France, though as a result of the re-emphasis on landing operations and the annual fleet exercises held on Culebra and Oahu from 1922 to 1925, a shift toward studying such operations as the British amphibious landings or raids at Gallipoli, Ostend, and Zeebrugge during World War I received further impetus. Select Marine officers, such as future General Oliver P. Smith (commander of the lst Marine Division during the Korean War 1950–51), LtGen Charles Barrett, who assisted in the writing of the rough draft of the *Tentative Landing Manual* in 1931–3 at Quantico, BrigGens Robert H. Dunlap (who tragically died before class convened in Paris in May 1931), and Lester A. Dessez, attended the prestigious French *École Superieure de Guerre*. In short, MajGen Lejeune and his successors believed that an educated officer corps was not only the key to the Corps' force modernization, but, more importantly, in the assumption of the landing operations mission.

Despite the severe cutbacks in manpower and austere budgets the Marine Corps suffered during the Great Depression and the administration of Herbert Hoover, who was no friend to the Marine Corps, Lejeune's successors made do with what little they had, and still trained a combat-ready force. One important change, however, was in the advancement and retention of officers. In order to reduce the backlog in promotions, and remove both the unfit and pre-World War I 'hump' of senior officers that had clogged the advancement of younger, more professionally competent officers schooled in the ways of modern combined arms warfare, MajGen Russell adopted promotion by selection and merit in 1935, despite the howls and protests of those senior officers who felt betrayed for their years of dedicated service to the country and the Marine Corps.

In 1935 MajGen Russell likewise adopted a better method in recruiting young men to the Marine Corps officer ranks directly from civilian life, and in conformity with the manpower limits placed upon HQMC by a budget and isolationist-minded Congress. Introduced during the summer of 1935, HQMC organized special camps or classes known as a Platoon Leader's Class or PLC, whereby young college-age men joined the Marine Corps Reserve and attended two six-week camps at Quantico between their sophomore and junior year, and junior and senior years, whereby, following graduation and successful completion of the training, they would be commissioned as second lieutenants in the Marine Corps Reserve. One such officer was Colonel Paul Sackett, who was a member of the first PLC class in 1935, and rose to the rank of colonel by the end of World War II. Colonel Sackett, who commanded a combat engineer battalion during World War II, recalled that the training in those days was 'tough though very professional', and that it prepared him for the rigours of combat in the Central Pacific during the war.

As the Marine Corps shifted its focus away from its emphasis on 'small wars' or counter-guerrilla operations to amphibious operations, the curriculum in all of the officers' courses at the Marine Corps Schools at Quantico began to reflect this important change in direction and emphasis. Despite the focus on amphibious operations at the MCS, Major General Commandant (1936–1943) Thomas Holcomb, in order to secure necessary funds from Congress, started at Quantico, as part of the MCS, an Officers' Base Defense School, which concentrated on defensive as opposed to offensive warfare, centered on defensive weapons systems (anti-aircraft, anti-ship, and artillery), searchlights, and so forth. Sergeant Carl Seaberg, who had been stationed at the

MCS in 1937 as a graphics artist, recalled that the officers, (primarily a young Major by the name of David M. Shoup, who would win the Medal of Honor at Tarawa in November 1943 and later become Commandant of the Marine Corps (1959–1963)), 'studied artillery, mathematics and trajectory at the MCS, and would rarely bother us clerks unless they needed something.' Yet when funds permitted, the emphasis remained squarely on amphibious warfare and landing operations, and to this end Marine officers continued to study combined arms warfare from World War I, as well as the lessons from the fleet exercises held once again in 1932 and subsequently, up to the eve of the US entry into World War II, at the Marine Barracks, New River, NC.

Despite the Depression, austere budgets, a hostile Chief Executive (President Herbert Hoover), and Army Chief of Staff (Gen Douglas MacArthur), both of whom favoured absorption of the Marines into the Army, MajGens Fuller, Russell, and Holcomb nonetheless managed to 'keep the Corps afloat', and turned inward to help further the development of amphibious warfare and officer and enlisted

---

Below: A Marine 60mm (2.36in) mortar crew trains at Camp Lejeune, NC, in mid-1943. As Marine tactical doctrine developed during the war, firepower and its application became increasingly important, and this was reflected in Marine training.

professional education. Even with a decline in manpower, reduced training schedules (recruit training dipped to as low as four weeks, with an average of 15 to 20 recruits per platoon), the Marine Corps awaited better days with an improved officer promotion and selection method, as well as a solid core of professional non-commissioned officers that would assist in the preparation of the Corps for war in 1941.

THE TEST OF WAR: ENLISTED AND OFFICER GROUND COMBAT TRAINING, 1939–1945

On 8 September 1939, just seven days after the outbreak of war in Europe on 1 September, President Franklin D. Roosevelt raised the authorized strength of the US Marine Corps to 25,000 officers and enlisted men. On that same day, the Commandant, MajGen Thomas Holcomb, immediately informed the Recruiting Service that all quotas on the number of men enlisted had been lifted. By February 1940, five months after the quotas had been lifted, Marine recruiters enlisted 7000 young men into the Marine Corps where for the same period a year earlier the number had been a dismal figure of 5861 recruits! Thus began the Marine Corps' wartime expansion, that would not end until the war's end in 1945. This rapid build-up so strained the training facilities that a modification of the recruit training system had to be enacted, with the eight week training cycle reduced to four weeks. With intuitive foresight, HQMC had planned for just such a reduction. Major General

Commandant Holcomb had issued orders as early as 1 June 1939, that effectively cut the schedule down to three weeks of intensive training that included both Saturdays and Sundays. Included in this training were two weeks' indoctrination and basic instruction in the 'School of the Soldier', followed by a third week of weapons training; care and use of the rifle and pistol, instruction in hand and rifle grenades, and whenever practical, instruction or demonstration of other infantry weapons were to be included in the final week.

As could be expected, the diminished time in recruit training resulted in a less-than-prepared Marine for the rigours of the Fleet Marine Force, particularly in rifle qualification and marksmanship training, a problem that had occurred during the 1920s when, in the rush to field expeditionary forces to both China and Nicaragua, HQMC cut into the recruit training schedules and eliminated or greatly curtailed marksmanship and the 'School of the Soldier', with the result that Marines had difficulties in Nicaragua in handling infantry weapons such as BARs, hand and rifle grenades, and Thompson sub-machine guns, as well as with basic marksmanship. In order to avoid similar problems in marksmanship, MajGen Holcomb issued a training memorandum that encouraged the recruit depot commanders to increase, as opposed to decrease, the amount of time allotted to rifle qualification and infantry weapons familiarization. Despite these and other shortcomings, the four week schedule remained in place for the rest of 1939, until

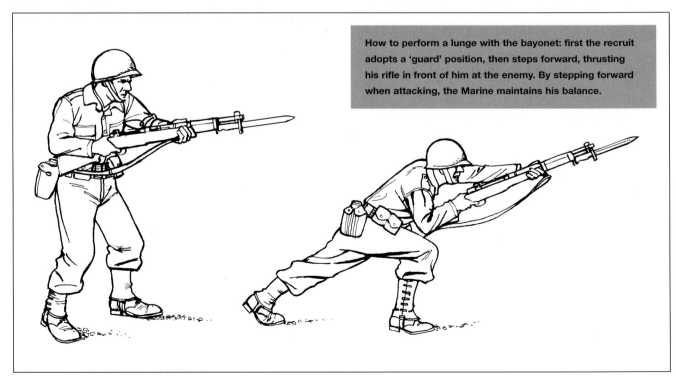

How to perform a lunge with the bayonet: first the recruit adopts a 'guard' position, then steps forward, thrusting his rifle in front of him at the enemy. By stepping forward when attacking, the Marine maintains his balance.

MARINE CORPS FLEET EXERCISES 1924–1941

March 1923 **Panama Canal, CZ**
A detachment of Marines conducted a series of landing operations in Panama then launched a mock attack against the Canal itself. Tested defences of the Canal, naval gunnery, ship-to-shore communications, and joint air defence doctrine with that of the Army. Fleet Problem No 2.

January 1924 **Culebra, Puerto Rico**
Members of the Marine Corps' East Coast Expeditionary Force commanded by BrigGen Eli K. Cole and Col Dion Williams participated in the annual fleet exercises to test Advanced Base Concept. Fleet Problem No 4. Exercise also held off Panama Canal.

March–April 1925 **Oahu, TH**
1500 Marines of Marine Corps West and East Coast Expeditionary Force join in combined Army–Navy exercise testing defences of US Army and Navy bases to resist enemy attack; also to test 'seizure' portion of advanced base exercise.

January 1932 **Oahu, TH**
First exercise held since 1925. To test landing boats, and naval gunfire.

February 13–14 1935 **Culebra, PR**
Objectives included testing Naval Gunfire Practices against land targets, and to give the officers and men training in embarkation procedures and landing operations. FLEX No 1.

12 January–17 February 1936 **Culebra, PR**
Objective was to establish, maintain and coordinate the signal agencies of the battalion. FLEX No 2.

February 1937 **San Clemente, CA**
Advanced Base Problem tested Naval Gunfire, embarkation and debarkation procedures. FLEX No 3.

13 January–15 March 1938 **Culebra, Puerto Rico**
Objective of this exercise was to test and demonstrate the effectiveness of air spotting in designating a group of targets; demonstration of command and control of air and ground spotting for naval gunfire and air support; demonstration of effectiveness of ship and fire control without previous knowledge of the range and bearing of the targets and without detailed plans of manoeuvre. FLEX No 4.

12 January–19 March 1939 **Culebra, PR**
Landing craft, primarily Higgins Boats and Bureau Boats, are tested. FLEX No 5.

15 Feb–8 Mar 1940 **Culebra, PR**
Exercise tested night landings; insertion of reconnaissance teams; command and control of naval gunfire; types of ammunition to be used in naval gunfire; assault craft waves and formations; landing craft tested. FLEX No 6.

4–16 Feb 1941 **Culebra, PR**
Joint Army-Marine landing exercise; first employment of assault transports; staff training procedures for Army and Marine officers during amphibious operations. FLEX No 7.

July–August 1941 **New River, NC***
Joint Army-Marine landing operations. Landing procedures; landing craft, and tactical training; small unit training.

* Renamed Camp Lejeune, N.C. in honor of Lieutenant General John A. Lejeune who died in November 1942.

March 1940 when the Major General Commandant, due to concerns over the requirements for the proper training of a Marine recruit, ordered the recruit depots to institute a seven week recruit training schedule, which had more marksmanship and field training allocated, and remained in place throughout World War II.

By the end of 1940, both Marine Corps Recruit Depots (MCRDs) at Parris Island, SC, and San Diego, CA, were operating at full capacity, as the Corps continued to expand on a daily basis. By the time of the Japanese attack on Pearl Harbor, the recruit depots and their respective infrastructure had, in fact, expanded tenfold, with a full-fledged training establishment in place to meet the next major expansion in the Marine Corps, that by the war's end would number 465,000 men and women.

Eventually, as the war progressed into 1944, HQMC returned to an eight-week recruit training schedule, due to the requirements for better-trained Marines, and the expected invasion of the Japanese home islands in 1945. To this end, the revised training schedule contained an increase in the amount of physical training to 38 hours at Parris Island and 40 hours at San Diego, and rifle marksmanship to 147 hours at the former, while the latter's increased to 112 hours. The 'School of the Soldier' or infantry skills received a slight increase as well. In short, HQMC had already anticipated the necessity of training more Marines for combat.

Officer Training

From the late 1920s through the 1930s to the eve of the US entrance into World War II, Marine officer training increased in both depth and in scope. While the peacetime officer training programmes had been geared toward the production of a small, highly competent professional officer corps, the lessons of Nicaragua in the use and employment of small arms necessitated a return to teaching the basic infantry skills to both junior and senior company grade officers (2nd and 1st

Above: All Marines are trained as infantrymen. Here, Marines in advanced individual training practice cross a stream during manoeuvres whilst wearing combat equipment. High levels of fitness were required for operations in the humid Pacific heat.

lieutenants and captains). Newly-commissioned officers attended first the Basic School, located at the Marine Barracks, Philadelphia, PA, where they studied drills and ceremonies, marksmanship, naval law, small arms training, minor tactics, and 'other subjects designed to prepare new officers for duty with all Corps activities'.

Company grade officers attended advanced schooling at either the Company Officers' Course or the US Army's

MARINE RECRUIT TRAINING SEVEN WEEK SCHEDULE, 1940–1944	
Major Subject Breakdown	*Training Hours*
Physical Training	100
Drill	44
Interior Guard	9
Guard	2
Military Courtesy	3
Bayonet Instruction	8
Musketry	2
Rifle Instruction	3
Field Training	72

Including: Patrolling, Scouting, Hikes, Marches, Signals, First Aid, Chemical Warfare, Cover and Concealment, Combat Principles.

Infantry Officers' Course at Fort Benning, GA, where the emphasis centered on infantry tactics, weapons employment, combined arms, and heavy weapons. Field grade officers attended either the Field Officers' Course at Quantico or the Army School of the Line or Command and Staff Colleges at Fort Leavenworth, KS, where senior first lieutenants to majors were 'taught the art of command; a thorough understanding of naval and military strategy and tactics in the national policies they tend to support; and a good working acquaintance with world politics and history . . . .' Colonels and lieutenant colonels attended the higher echelon war colleges of both the US Navy and Army, the Army Industrial College, or in some cases, the *École Superieure de Guerre* in Paris, France, until France went to war against Germany in 1939 after the invasion of Poland.

Besides attending special courses offered by the Army or Navy technical schools (Signals, Cavalry, Ordnance, Infantry, Coast Artillery, Engineer, Chemical and Gas, Quartermaster, and Artillery), while Navy schools included Radio Engineering, and Flight School at Pensacola, FA, the only 'Marine Corps School' that taught clearly 'Marine-oriented subjects' was the Base Defense Weapons Course. The course, a part of the MCS at Quantico, had been designed to train Marine company officers in the use of weapons in the defense of advanced naval bases, and light field artillery (5in (127mm) naval guns). As discussed above, the Base Defense Weapons Course in time became the primary source for artillery officers for the brigades of the Fleet Marine Force.

When it became obvious to officials at HQMC that the Army schools could not produce the number of trained engineers or other specialists necessary for Marine Corps requirements, it began to establish its own schools at first at the Army base itself and then eventually all at Quantico. The only school not co-located at Quantico was the Amphibian Tractor Officers' Course, which remained at Dunedin, FA. Nonetheless, Marine officers still attended Army and Navy schools, as well as specialist civilian schools for aviators, such as the Massachusetts Institute of Technology and the Sperry Gyroscope Company.

Starting in 1940, with the limited call up of the Marine Corps Reserve, reserve officers in need of refresher training attended special camps at Quantico, VA, in order to bring them up to date in their respective military occupation skills. Also, in order to train more officers quickly for the expansion of the Regular Marine Corps, HQMC initiated its first of several Reserve Officers' Courses (ROC) at Quantico when, starting on 1 November 1940, candidates arrived and began an intensive period of training that lasted anywhere from 13 to 16 weeks. Due to the fact that many of the candidates had been literally plucked from civilian universities and colleges, many had no formal military training, which necessitated a longer, more intense individualistic period of training. Nonetheless, the ROC candidates proved adept, and in time produced fine combat officers.

In time, the ROC classes produced 1089 Marine officers that included Officers' Candidate Courses (OCC which had been made up of former enlisted men and college graduates), PLC, and ROC candidates. Many of these same officers led the first contingent of Marines ashore on Guadalcanal, and by the time of the Central Pacific drive had proven themselves effective combat leaders trained in a wide variety of combat-related fields and specialities. As occurred in World War I, however, the vast majority of Marine junior officers during World War II once again came from the ranks of outstanding enlisted men who were given temporary wartime commissions, and proved to be effective and extremely competent combat platoon and company-grade leaders.

Below: Marines practice an amphibious assault during the latter stages of World War II by disembarking from a Navy Landing Ship Tank (LST). Note the wrapping used to protect their rifles from the effects of salt water.

COMBAT AND COMBAT REPLACEMENT TRAINING 1942–1945

After the first combat actions on Guadalcanal in August and September 1942, HQMC made the decision to open a replacement training centre on the island of Samoa, where newly-graduated Marines coming from New River, NC, received an eight-week intensive training with classes in cover and concealment, field fortifications, sniper tactics and countermeasures, infantry weapons and employment, physical conditioning, acclimatization procedures, jungle warfare, small unit tactics, and amphibious training. This training was broken up into two four-week periods, where Marines first received individual basic skills and then progressive field training that included night and jungle training. Marine officers likewise stressed amphibious embarkation and disembarkation procedures, weapons firing and training, with classes and field training in battalion and regimental weapons.

As more and more Marines returned from combat operations in the Solomons (1942–43), training intensified, with more emphasis placed on infantry skills, particularly on weapons and weapons employment. As the fighting for the Marines shifted from the jungles of the Northern Solomons to the Central Pacific, the lessons learned on Tarawa, coupled with a change in Japanese tactics, forced changes in the training programme from jungle warfare to that of an emphasis on small unit tactics centered on the use of hand and rifle grenades, flamethrowers, and explosives, all of which now received top priority as Marine planners aimed at the heart of the Japanese defensive ring in the Marianas, Marshalls, Palau, and Ryukus Islands. More important was the extension of the replacement training cycle from eight to twelve weeks. For infantry specialists, HQMC directed that the first four weeks were to 'be devoted to basic infantry training, while the remaining eight weeks were to be devoted to specialist training in the weapon to which the individual was assigned'. Riflemen and Marines whose weapon was the BAR attended a straight twelve-week course.

Lengthened Syllabus

For the riflemen and BAR men, the new syllabus included 720 hours of instruction as compared to the previous 409 hours under the old eight-week schedule. Additional instruction included joint exercises with supporting weapons such as machine guns, mortars, artillery, and in preparation for fighting on the Japanese home islands, fighting in semi-urban areas such as villages and small towns. With the dropping of classes in jungle warfare, Marines received classes in light machine guns, the 60mm (2.36in) mortar, and 2.36in (60mm) rocket launchers. Anti-tank gunners, mortarmen, and machine gunners likewise received an increase from 218 to 484 hours in weapons handling and employment classes. With the bulk of the instructors in these classes coming from combat veterans, both officers and enlisted men assigned to instructor duty attended what has been described as a 'super infantry school', where they received a thorough course of instruction in infantry warfare. In addition to this emphasis on individual training, Marines attending replacement training received intensive classes in fire team, squad, and platoon tactics, with emphasis placed on bunker and emplacement reduction.

By the time of the campaigns on Iwo Jima (19 February–26 March 1945) and Okinawa (April–June 1945), Marines had been well-trained in the infantry and combined arms assault techniques pioneered on Tarawa in November 1943, and implemented them with deadly effect on the bloody ridges of Peleliu in September 1944.

In short, as occurred during World War I, Marine training in the 1920s

Left: Marines practice assembly and disassembly of a .30in (7.62mm) calibre Browning light machine gun whilst on their way to perform another amphibious landing.

Above: The tension shows on the faces of these Marines as they anxiously await to go ashore during an amphibious landing on Iwo Jima in February 1945. The attack on Iwo Jima proved to be a bitter and bloody experience for the US forces.

through to the end of World War II constantly adapted to the needs placed upon it. From the jungles of the West Indies to Nicaragua in the 1920s, the Marine Corps Schools and training depots rapidly sought to include the lessons of infantry warfare and the employment of combined arms into Marine training. As Marines returned from expeditionary duty in the early 1930s, the emphasis once again shifted to training Marines in amphibious techniques and basic and unit infantry skills. While enlisted Marines trained in the foothills of San Diego, CA, and on Culebra, Puerto Rico, Guantanamo Bay, Cuba, and at Quantico, Marine officers and staff non-commissioned officers attended Infantry Weapons Schools at Quantico. Other Marine officers attended Army schools and exercised on the beaches of San Clemente, CA, and New River, NC, and added to the collective body of knowledge of infantry and combined arms lessons learned and employed by Marines during World War I.

In fact, much of the fighting in the Central Pacific, and on the Japanese home islands of Iwo Jima and Okinawa, took on the resemblance of the fighting that took place in France in 1918, hence vindicating the proponents of such training and inculcation at the MCS in the 1920s and 1930s. Indeed, much of what the Marine Corps did during the early days of its hectic preparations when the US declared war on Japan on 8 December 1941, resembled the efforts undertaken by another generation of Marines during World War I. This included the training and recruitment of enlisted men and officers, educating and drilling them, and in the preparation for the amphibious warfare of the jungles of the Solomon Islands to the coral atolls of the Central Pacific and volcanic soil of Iwo Jima. Tied in directly with the training of a US Marine during this period were the innovative techniques applied by Marines as the Japanese Army shifted from linear, jungle-oriented warfare, to the non-linear defensive strategy of drawing an enemy inland and allowing him to attrite himself as he assaulted in force from the sea. As the Marines demonstrated in assault after assault in the Pacific War, the flexibility afforded to them by amphibious warfare permitted adaption techniques and a tactical system that was both innovative and highly destructive, and in the end resulted in the annihilation of Japanese forces in battle after battle during World War II.

CHAPTER 4

Marine Battlefield Tactics and Techniques 1942–1945

The Marine Corps initially based its training for the fighting in the Pacific in World War II on its experiences in France in World War I. However, as the Japanese switched to a defensive style of fighting, the Marines proved flexible enough to evolve into an excellent combined arms fighting unit.

US MARINE CORPS battlefield tactics and techniques used during World War II evolved not only from its experiences in World War I and expeditionary duty on Hispaniola and Nicaragua (1915–1933), but from actual combat during the length of the war in the Pacific up through the Okinawa campaign in April 1945. In fact, many of the techniques employed by Marines after 1943 came as a result of the tactical reorganization of the Marine Corps' basic fighting units, ranging from the fire team to the regiment, from late 1943 until February 1945. This chapter is an analysis of not only how Marines operated tactically on the battlefields of the Pacific theatre, and how they successfully adjusted their tactics to meet and achieve operational objectives as the war shifted from the jungles of the Solomons to the coral atolls and islands of the Central Pacific, but how they responded to the Japanese Army's shift from a linear on-line defence, to that of a modified defence in depth from 1944 to the end of the war. The Marine Corps response to these changes illustrated the tactical flexibility of Marine rifle regiments and battalions that could effectively employ combined arms (the infantry-tank-artillery team) against a determined adversary, a flexibility instilled during the interwar era that matured and blossomed during World War II.

Left: During a lull in fighting, a Marine rests on top of Mount Suribachi on Iwo Jima in February 1945, looking down on the landing beach below. Various support ships can clearly be seen unloading stores and equipment.

Lessons of World War I, 1919–1941

While Marine Brigadier General Lester A. Dessez asserted, when a student at the Marine Corps' Company Officers Course in the early 1920s to (then) BrigGen Ben H. Fuller, who was Commandant, Marine Corps Schools at Quantico, VA, that 'World War I will never be fought again', the fighting that raged on the coral atolls and on such places as Iwo Jima and Okinawa came very close to resembling the type of fighting leathernecks endured during the summer and autumn of 1918. Fighting over a wasteland devastated by shells and gunfire, raked by machine gun bullets and sprayed by flamethrowers, and advancing against an enemy dug in deep into the ground, the battlefields of France provided future Marine leaders with an idea of how a land war might evolve during the initial stages when seizing an advanced naval base. In fact, the experience that Marine leaders such as Major General John A. Lejeune, Lieutenant Colonel Thomas Holcomb, Major Earl H. Ellis, and Captain Holland M. 'Howlin Mad' Smith came away with from World War I served them well in preparing Marines for the island war during World War II in the Pacific.

The most important lesson for their future strategy that Marines carried with them from the battlefields of France back to Quantico was the employment of combined arms, then centered on infantry, artillery, and machine guns. In fact, in a post-battle synopsis of the fighting around Belleau Wood, MajGen Lejeune recounted that if World War I proved anything, the battlefield had been dominated by the artillery and machine gun, and in assault after assault, 'Again, was decisively shown the great importance of artillery to infantry. Infantry alone without material, makes little progress. If the enemy combines personnel and material, we must do the same or lose the game.' In a direct parallel to the fighting on Tarawa (1943) and later during the savage fighting on Saipan and Peleliu in 1944, and on Iwo Jima and Okinawa in 1945, the Marine Brigade lost 112 officers and 4598 men in one month's fighting in Belleau Wood. With such losses, and with the nature of the open warfare fighting that General John J. Pershing and other American commanders insisted upon, Marine officers concluded at the war's end that the battles they participated in during the fighting offered many lessons for the operational and tactical nature of future wars. In fact, the US Army later incorporated many of these same lessons in its 1923 Field Service Regulations (FSRs) and Infantry Drill Regulations (IDRs) that Marines studied and trained by during the interwar era. Thus when the US Marines Corps entered World War II, many of its senior officers had either seen combat in France during the last war, or had been well-grounded in the tactical and doctrinal lessons of that war,

as found later in the US Army's landmark 1923 FSRs and IDRs. As the nature of the fighting shifted from the jungles of the Solomon Islands to the coral atolls and volcanic islands of the Central Pacific, the fighting came to resemble more and more that endured by the Marines during World War I.

JUNGLE FIGHTING AND SMALL UNIT OPERATIONS, 1942–1943

For Marines, Guadalcanal was a war of small unit operations. Indeed, many of the tactical innovations used by the Marines had been used by their predecessors in France, in Central America, primarily in Nicaragua, and on the islands of Haiti and the Dominican Republic during the interwar era. Even with the deployment to China in the 1920s and 1930s, as Marines guarded the US legation's compound, the leathernecks developed the basic tactical formation of a rifle company comprised of three rifle platoons composed of six fighting teams of four Marines each. Each fire team was led by a senior private or junior non-commissioned officer, and due to its tactical flexibility could be employed in an independent action. Upon the expansion of the

One- or two-man foxholes gave Marines protection against sudden Japanese *banzai* attacks or artillery fire. The foxholes were intended to protect most of a Marine's body whilst allowing him to aim and fire his weapon easily.

One-man
foxhole

Two-man
foxhole

Above: A Marine rifle squad fords a stream on Guadalcanal in mid-August 1942. For the Marines, jungle conditions such as this were common in the early part of the war, before the fighting moved to open coral atolls such as Tarawa.

Marine Corps, however, and with the issuance of the E-Tables of Organization, the Marine rifle team went from four to six men, with the average Marine squad being twelve Marines: squad leader, six riflemen, and two BAR and two assistant BAR men, all armed with M-1 Garands or BARs. All Marine formations had been organized on the triangular organization of three squads per platoon, three platoons per company, three companies per battalion, and three battalions per regiment, and finally three regiments plus supporting arms per division.

Guadalcanal

Tactically, the Guadalcanal campaign vindicated Marine training, which focused on small unit operations with the emphasis being on initiative and tactical flexibility. Thus, the tactics employed by Marines were primarily lineal in nature due to the defensive nature of the campaign. According to Sergeant George MacGillivray, who served on a 37mm (1.45in) gun crew, the nature of the fighting usually involved units no larger than companies and as small as squads. In fact, for the Marines who fought there two

decades later, Guadalcanal closely resembled Vietnam, which was also a war waged by small units. Marines, armed with rifles, bayonets, hand grenades, mortars, machine guns, and 37mm anti-tank guns – used primarily as anti-personnel weapons and normally against bunkers – fought off daily Japanese banzai attacks or sought out the elusive Japanese snipers, and engaged in constant patrolling. From the start, Marine infantry and artillery commanders effectively used the terrain on Guadalcanal to their advantage in order to maximize the effectiveness of their weapons. Thus, Marine positions were usually dug in and anchored along the rivers and ravines that bisected the main line of resistance located at Henderson Airfield, and allowed the leathernecks to effectively employ all of their firepower.

Marines on Guadalcanal and on Tulagi likewise developed countermeasures to deal with Japanese positions carved into the sides of ridge lines and in caves. As would be the case later in the war on Peleliu, Iwo Jima, and Okinawa, Marines belonging to the 1st Raider Battalion, commanded by Colonel Merritt A. Edson, spent the majority of the fighting on Guadalcanal and Tulagi destroying Japanese machine guns that had been built inside the mouths of caves, blasting them with satchel charges of dynamite and explosives or canisters of gasoline with grenades attached.

Marine First Lieutenant Herbert L. Merillat provided an excellent description of the type of fighting experienced by

Marines on Tulagi, that underscored the tactics employed by Marines there in combating the Japanese:

'... the Japs holed up in caves in the sides of hills. It is a small island only about two miles long, and there is a ridge line along the northern part of the island and a high hill forms the southern end. The Japanese defenses were concentrated on that hill. It took two days of bitter fighting to clean up all the Japs who had taken to caves in those hills and in the gulleys below the hills. Often large groups of Japs got into one cave through a narrow entrance. As one runner at the mouth of the cave would be picked off by Marines, another would take his place, and so on until every Jap in the cave had been killed. I believe only four prisoners were taken on Tulagi. And the rest of the Japs were killed except for some who may have escaped to Florida, a nearby island, under the cover of night.'

Master Gunnery Sergeant Ray Stock, who served with the 2nd Battalion, 7th Marine Regiment, and landed on Gavutu and later Tananboga, as the main units of the 1st Marine Division landed on Guadalcanal, recalled that the fighting on both islands was 'savage'. Stock specifically remembered that the Marines had to battle with the Japanese who had holed themselves up in the caves and hills of Tananboga. The Japanese, Sgt Stock remembered, 'could direct a plunging fire down from the holes in the hill and their machine gunners caught our boats before they ever landed'. After the fighting on Guadalcanal and its adjacent islands, 1stLt Merillat stated that the Marines now had a foretaste 'of what lay in store for us in the future'.

Developing Tactics

The fighting for the Northern Solomon Island of New Georgia 'gave impetus to a new set of ground tactics that emphasized close tank infantry coordination'. The experiences on New Georgia 'pointed to the need for the infantry to be supported by heavier tanks and tank-mounted flamethrowers'. The fighting there also revealed the inherent weaknesses of the light tanks (primarily M3 Stuarts) in destroying the well-fortified Japanese bunkers. Perhaps the most important lessons Marines gained from the fighting in the Solomons from 1942 up to the Bougainville campaign were, however, methods in patrolling, and the familiarization of the adjacent organization's mission in order to ensure continuity, as well as a thorough indoctrination of assault techniques on enemy bunkers. Marine Major Lewis W. Walt provided an excellent reason for this: 'As in the Basic Field Manual, each man should know the objective . . . . keep 'em in squad columns, with two scouts in front of each squad. . . . This method, we have found, insures control.'

Above: A Marine examines a Japanese bunker on Peleliu in September 1944. By late 1943 the Japanese changed their tactics, using bunkers and prepared positions to hinder the US forces in their efforts to recapture Japanese conquests.

Tactically, during the fighting on Bougainville, the 3rd Marine Division developed a formation which it called 'contact imminent', which Marines of this division employed for an approach march through the jungle to enemy positions. This formation ensured a 'Steady and controlled advance, had several variations and consisted of a march column of units which had flank guards deployed to cover the widest possible front under existing conditions of visual or physical contact.' Spearheaded by a security patrol, it avoided all trains, with the Marine squad controlled by a field telephone that kept in constant contact with headquarters. The officer or non-commissioned officer at the head of the main body controlled the speed and direction of the column. A formation employing the 'contact imminent' could move at a rate of 500 yards per hour in swamps and heavy foliage. This formation also afforded maximum protection to its members in that it could 'fend off small enemy attacks without a delay in its forward movement.' It was also flexible enough that it permitted the squad or platoon leader enough time to deploy his Marines for immediate combat on the flanks, on line, or toward the rear of the formation.

One last form of fighting used by the Marines on Guadalcanal and in New Georgia that deserves special mention was the use of the bayonet. Marines had been particularly well trained in the use of the bayonet since, as a training memorandum suggested, it inspired an 'aggressiveness' by its user, and tended to keep him on the offensive. During the 1920s and 1930s Marine training emphasized the use of the bayonet in close-in combat. In fact, in training manual after training manual during the interwar era, the terms 'will to meet and destroy the enemy', the 'spirit of the bayonet', and so forth frequently appeared to underscore the use of cold steel in battle. Marines learned how to use the bayonet starting from the time they entered the Marine Corps, and it continued to be an important feature in their preparation for combat in the Pacific during World War II. Marines used the bayonet at 'night, on infiltration missions, and whenever secrecy had to be observed.' For the leathernecks, 'The bayonet was the weapon of silence and surprise.' Likewise, as Marines experienced throughout the war in the Pacific, firepower alone often failed to drive the Japanese out of their defensive positions, and thus necessitated the use of the bayonet in hand-to-hand combat.

Bayonet Techniques

Essentially, Marines were taught three basic positions when employing bayonets: (1) 'Guard', in order to defend oneself; (2) 'Short Guard', normally used when passing through short woods, around buildings, and through trenches, or when enemy contact is expected suddenly and at close quarters, or (3) 'High Port', used for immediate self-defence

or expected enemy contact. Marine bayonet training consisted of the 'Whirl', 'Long Thrust', and 'Withdrawal from Long Thrust', all of which were taught to be short, violent actions necessitating a steady hand and quick reflexes. They also learned how to 'parry right', 'parry left', and do 'vertical and horizontal butt strokes', with both their rifles and bayonets. Besides individual bayonet training, Marines likewise received instruction in the group's use of the bayonet. In short, despite the advent of semi-automatic weapons, the bayonet remained the primary weapon for teaching and retaining the 'offensive' spirit in Marines.

One last lesson learned by the Marines in the jungle fighting during the Solomons campaign was the use of fighting positions such as the one- and two-man foxholes. Built primarily for cover and concealment, these positions offered some measure of protection against Japanese infiltrators during the night, and served as ideal fighting positions during a Japanese banzai attack.

Below: A Marine gives a wounded leatherneck a drink of water from his canteen during the fighting on Peleliu. The attritional nature of the fighting led to casualties, despite the Marines' attempts to offset this with the use of greater firepower.

By the end of the fighting in the Northern Solomons Marines had gathered a considerable 'bookful of lessons' learned while fighting the Japanese forces in the jungles of Guadalcanal, New Georgia, Bougainville, and on New Britain. Marines discovered that the lessons of the fighting experienced in Central America in the interwar period remained valid, particularly in regard to use of automatic weapons and their rapid rates of fire, which proved extremely useful in firefights against the Japanese in close-in combat. By the time the Marines landed on New Britain on 26 December 1943, they had perfected night patrolling, and close-in fighting over so-called 'brush-choked terrain', where some of the bitterest fighting in the South Pacific took place against the remnants of the Imperial Japanese Army in the Solomons area.

'BUNKER BUSTING' AND A CHANGE IN TACTICS

Even while Marines fought the tenacious Japanese Army in the swamps of Bougainville, Admiral Chester Nimitz's Central Pacific Drive began with the Marine assault on Tarawa, which was the first successful, and perhaps most costly, amphibious assault on a Japanese-held island. In three days of relentless fighting, Marine riflemen, tankers, and combat engineers burned, blasted, and finally eliminated an enemy determined to fight to the death. Tarawa was, as a Marine post-battle report concluded, 'a battle where perseverance dominated over adversity, where individual courage and collective know how defeated a strong Japanese garrison on its own ground and in its own positions.'

Marines who participated in the assault on Tarawa's Betio atoll, a part of the Gilbert Islands, cited that the main factor for the success of the Tarawa landing was the pre-invasion training they had received 'in coordinating their employment of demolitions, flamethrowers, and firepower in knocking out the coconut palm log, coral, and concrete bunkers and pillboxes'. The fighting on Tarawa closely resembled the fighting on Tulagi during the Guadalcanal campaign, with Marine rifle teams inching their way forward against murderous machine gun and mortar fire that came from the many dug-in concrete emplacements that the Japanese Special Naval Landing Forces (Marines) manned and died in – almost to a man. Rear Admiral Meichi Shibasaki, who made Tarawa virtually 'impregnable' and had boasted prior to the invasion that 'a million Americans couldn't take Tarawa in a 100 years', attempted to make good on his pledge as he and 4690 of his Tarawa garrison died, and made the

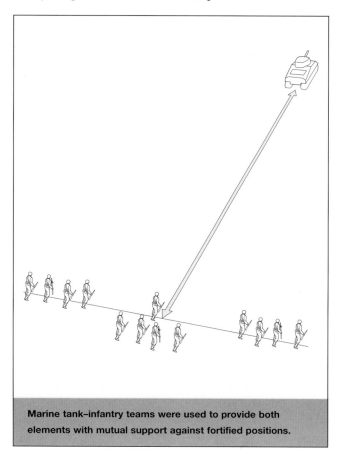

Marine tank–infantry teams were used to provide both elements with mutual support against fortified positions.

The correct position for firing a rifle grenade. Rifle grenades were used to destroy Japanese bunkers.

Above: Japanese bunkers, like the one shown above, proved a formidable obstacle to the Marines, as their construction forced the adoption of new tactics. Tanks, artillery, explosives and flamethrowers were all used against them by the Marines.

Americans pay in blood for every inch of Betio taken by the assaulting Marines.

The Marines' success on Tarawa nonetheless pointed to some problems that had to be overcome prior to the assault on the Marshalls (Roi-Namur, Kwajalein, and Eniwetok) and Mariana Islands (Saipan, Guam, and Tinian). These included tank–infantry coordination, use of demolitions (explosives), flamethrowers, and artillery in a coordinated assault. One of the major conclusions and an important lesson learned, and soon adopted, as Marines of the 4th Marine Division prepared to assault the Marshalls, was that all Marines, regardless of their specialities, had to know how to employ demolitions, which up to that time had been used exclusively by combat engineers.

As Marines prepared for the simultaneous assault set for 31 January 1944 on Roi-Namur, Kwajalein, and Eniwetok, the greatest emphasis was on the destruction of enemy pill-boxes. In order to facilitate this, each infantry regiment organized two assault demolition teams – which numbered about 20 infantrymen each – for use against these and other

fortified positions. Both types of team contained demolitions, bazooka, and BAR groups, with a flamethrower operator and his assistant as the nucleus of the first team, while a light machine gun served the same function in the second team. These two assault teams fulfilled the same function as engineer troops.

THE TANK–INFANTRY TEAM: 'BORN IN FIRE, BAPTIZED IN BLOOD'

One other lesson learned painfully on Tarawa was in tank–infantry coordination. As Marines discovered on New Georgia and in the early stages of the Tarawa landing, the tank could be a useful weapon if employed properly. Unfortunately, however, the armour on the M3 Stuart (British Honey) light tank, later replaced by the heavier M5 version, proved to be extremely vulnerable to the Japanese 75mm (2.95in) howitzers. On Tarawa, these same guns initially played havoc with Marine armour. Yet as Japanese defenders were eventually ground down by the Marine assault teams, the newer M4A2 Sherman proved to be an excellent troop infantry support weapon. Advancing slowly with Marine infantry, 'Time and again, Japanese emplacements of reinforced concrete, steel, and sand were reduced by direct fire from the tanks' main guns,' though one might

Above: A US Marine, armed with a Thompson sub-machine gun, fires on a suspected Japanese tunnel on Tarawa in November 1943. The firepower of weapons such as the Thompson gave the Marines an advantage in close-quarter fighting.

add that the accompanying Marine infantrymen assisted in the process of reducing the Japanese fortifications. The slower, much heavier armoured M4 Shermans with their 76mm (3in) main armament either fired directly into an enemy emplacement, or covered advancing Marine riflemen as they tossed grenades, satchel charges, and poured deadly napalm with flamethrowers into the Japanese fortifications. In short, 'tank–infantry tactics proved satisfactory, but only on level ground where the tanks could maneuver' against the entrenched Japanese defenders.

During subsequent operations on the Marshalls and especially on Saipan , the tank–infantry team came of age as M4 Shermans and Marine riflemen kept the assault elements – and attack itself – moving forward. As one HQMC after-action report stated: 'The technique of the tank–infantry teams pushing rapidly forward, closely followed by demolition and flamethrower teams is concurred in by this Headquarters as sound. However, emphasis is placed on the fact that it must be a continuous movement in which light enemy resistance is neutralized and bypassed by the forward

elements of the infantry–tank teams, then the supporting elements of the infantry equipped with demolitions and flamethrowers reduce these isolated enemy positions before they can recover and fire on the rear of our troops moving forward.'

The study continued: 'This technique is particularly effective in searching out the real strong points and thereby avoiding holding up the attack by weak and scattered resistance. When a strongpoint is encountered, the infantry–tank team and demolition–flame thrower team become integrated and operate together until the strong point is reduced.'

Mutual Support

The most important benefit besides its bunker-busting capability, was that the tank–infantry team was mutually supportive. Tanks protected the exposed infantrymen by providing effective suppressing fire from its main or coaxial machine guns, while on the other hand, infantrymen prevented Japanese suicide teams from first immobilizing and then destroying the tanks and killing its occupants. Infantrymen likewise knocked out lurking Japanese anti-tank guns and magnetic mines, which took a heavy toll of Marine tanks employed on New Georgia and in the Marshalls. In order to protect themselves against the mines laid by the Japanese, Marine tank crews placed oak planking on the bottom of the hull and on the exposed areas of their tanks.

In order to take full advantage of the manoeuvreability of the tank–infantry team concept, HQMC assigned each Marine regiment during the Saipan operation 18 Sherman tanks, plus a platoon of four 'flamethrower' tanks (the Canadian-built 'Ronsons'), and two light tanks. This concept allowed the accompanying tanks to improve steadily the inter-operability of the attacking infantry and supporting armour, who became familiarized with each other's operating procedures.

During the fighting on Okinawa, Marine commanders employed the tank–infantry teams in one of two ways. The first was the neutralization of an objective by supporting fire, with the ground troops armed with BARs, rifle grenades and flamethrowers, preceded by Sherman tanks-advancing to secure the area. This type of attack, however, proved effective only against those positions lightly defended by the enemy. When Marine commanders employed these tactics against more heavily-defended Japanese positions, the Japanese would often lay down a furious and voluminous barrage of fire on the attackers, which in turn pinned them down, and prevented them from either advancing forward or retreating. The second method, more widely used during the Okinawa campaign,

had Sherman tanks blasting away at suspected enemy caves and positions at close range in front of the general tank–infantry advance. 'Tanks and armoured flamethrowers (LVT-As) ranged out ahead of the front lines to distances up to 800 yards', destroying enemy positions on both the forward and reverse slopes by pointing their 75mm (2.95in) guns' point-blank fire and flame directly into the cave or emplacement. During the bitter fighting for Sugar Loaf Mountain, Marine tanks fought 'hull defilade' in order to deliver 'a flat trajectory fire' into the enemy's positions. Also, the M-7 'Priest', with its mobile 105mm (4.1in) howitzer, proved extremely effective as a close-in support weapon, directing point-blank fire against enemy caves and emplacements. In time, the M-7 became the most powerful organic weapon to a Marine rifle regiment.

As in Europe and Russia, tanks became ideal infantry carriers that could rush the foot-slogging infantry to the front of a critical area or, as was the case on Okinawa, could assist in the exploitation of a wavering enemy line of defence, and thus allow the Marines to follow through quickly with an

Below: A key instrument used in the destruction of Japanese positions was the flamethrower, a potent weapon that was much feared. Although its operators required close protection, it was capable of clearing bunkers and other positions in one burst.

attack. During the Okinawa campaign Private Jack Wiggins, who served with the 29th Marines during the fighting on the Oroku Peninsula and rode into battle atop a Sherman tank, stated: 'Once dismounted, we could then direct and exploit their firepower to the utmost against the Japs.'

Okinawa

It was on Okinawa, in fact, that Marines refined their tank–infantry tactics, and successfully employed two techniques that further enhanced the striking power of both these Marine arms. As the Marines pushed toward the southern part of the island, where the Japanese were dug in along the Shuri Castle line, its open-country terrain permitted a greater use of all three arms – tanks, artillery or mortars, and infantry.

Japanese defences on part of the island of Tarawa as identified by the intelligence section of the 2nd Marine Division prior to the attack on 20 November 1943. Every inch of the beach was covered by sandbags and barricades.

Supported by an attached Army 4.2in (107mm) mortar unit, which provided highly-effective suppressive firepower, the tanks of the 1st Marine Division and its supporting infantry were able to close in at greater quarters with the Japanese, and prevented them from using their suicide squads against the Marine tanks. In fact, working with Lieutenant Colonel 'Jeb' Stuart's 1st Tank Battalion, the Marines 'developed a new method of protecting tanks and reducing vulnerability to the infantry in the assault'. This method, according to Marine Colonel Wilburt S. Brown, 'placed an artillery observer in one of the tanks with a radio to one of the 155mm [6.1in] howitzer battalions. We'd also had an aerial observer overhead. We used 75mm [2.95in] pack [howitzers] and LVT-A's [armed with 75mm howitzers] that had an air burst capability. If any Jap [suicider] showed anywhere we opened fire with an air burst and kept a pattern of shell fragments patterning down around the tanks.' Marine tanks likewise shuttled fresh troops right to the front line by dropping them underneath the hull from inside the tank, as well as assisting in the evacuation of wounded Marines, placed aboard through the crew's escape

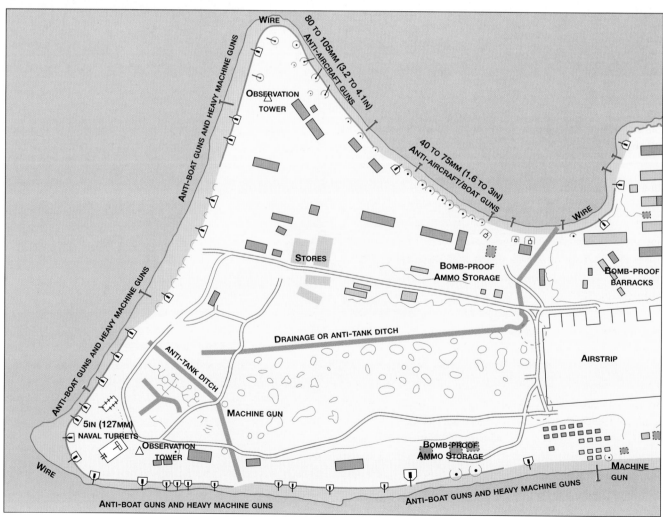

Above: A Marine tank–infantry team in action on Bougainville in mid-1943. Close cooperation between the tanks and Marines forged an effective combined arms team which was capable of dealing with most Japanese threats.

hatches in the bottom of the tank, or, less safely, strapped onto the outside of the tank.

Marine tanks played an important role in cracking the Japanese defensive line anchored on Kunishi Ridge through their elimination of Japanese General Ushijima's veteran front-line troops that had manned these positions. Also supporting the Marines was the M-7 Priest self-propelled 105mm (4.1in) howitzer, that added more firepower to a Marine assault with its ability to 'punch through' the many steel and concrete bunkers and pillboxes along the Shuri Castle–Sugar Loaf Mountain areas. On Okinawa, tanks functioned as the supreme 'direct-fire, close-in support weapon' for the assaulting infantry. Tanks could go where artillery couldn't, and destroy what the latter couldn't see.

By the battle's end, 51 Marine Shermans had been destroyed by Japanese artillery and anti-tank guns. Despite the fact that the Sherman found itself outgunned in Europe, at least by the more powerful German Tiger and Panther tanks, Marines skillfully employed their tanks very effec-

tively as infantry assault weapons. Furthermore, for those tanks disabled though not destroyed, Marine maintenance crews worked round the clock and restored practically every one of them, and, as a result of their ingenuity, 'the assault infantry battalions never lacked for armored firepower, mobility, and shock action. The concept of Marine combined-arms task forces was now well underway.'

'FIND'EM, FIX'EM, AND BLAST'EM' TACTICS, 1943–1945

In order to counter the overwhelming fire superiority of the Americans, the Japanese, starting on Guadalcanal, as 1stLt Herb Merillat recounted above, retreated to fixed positions and fortifications. This then involved both Marines and soldiers in a costly war of attrition that did not let up until the war's conclusion in August 1945. In fact, this strategy of attrition became evident as the earlier Japanese tactics of contesting the Marine's landings gave way to a defence-in-depth, with a series of interlocking fortifications and pillboxes built into a solid defensive network. This first became apparent on the islands of Tarawa, Saipan, and later on Peleliu, where Japanese *rikusentai* and soldiers forced the US Marines and soldiers to engage every pillbox in what

Above: A Marine 3.5in (89mm) rocket or 'bazooka' team takes aim at a Japanese position. By the war's end the Marines had refined the 'find'em, fix'em, and destroy them' tactics that saved many leathernecks' lives.

essentially became miniature set-piece battles reminiscent of the fighting on the Western Front during World War I – and in particular the Battle for Belleau Wood during the Chateau Thierry counter-offensive (5–26 June 1918), where the Marines and doughboys had to wipe out the German machine gun nests one by one. Bracketed by mortars, howitzers, and naval guns, and covered by machine guns, the Japanese had planned 'to defend Saipan from prepared positions on the beach and in the caves that were a prominent feature of the island'. As the tempo of the US advance increased, and taking lessons from their German allies, who had failed to stop the Allied assault at the beachheads at Normandy, the Japanese moved their positions inland with deadly consequences. Thus the Marines were forced to adapt to the changing tactical nature of the war, which in turn brought about the creation of select units, designated inside a Marine battalion and regiment, as assault troops equipped with flamethrowers, 37mm (1.45in) anti-tank guns, bazookas, dynamite, bangalore torpedoes, and satchel charges, in order to 'find'em, fix'em, and blast'em'.

The Role of Terrain

One last factor that influenced the formation of these special assault units was the terrain itself. As Marines discovered throughout the Pacific, the terrain often dictated tactics. This became especially true as the fighting shifted from the jungles and swamps of the Solomons to the jagged coral atolls of the Central Pacific. As mentioned above, the tables of organization in a Marine rifle company and battalion changed as the nature of the war shifted from close-in jungle warfare to the open warfare of the Central Pacific. In fact, a large portion of the tactics employed later on Iwo Jima and Okinawa stemmed from the bloody fighting that raged on Saipan and Peleliu.

It was after the bloody assault on Peleliu in September 1944 that Marine pre-invasion training began to emphasize 'bunker busting' techniques. This involved a close working relationship between all three (later four) arms – infantry, artillery, and tanks. In fact, as Marines prepared for the main assaults on the outer rings of the Japanese home islands of Iwo Jima and Okinawa, Capt George P. Hunt and LtCol Lewis W. Walt introduced a new course of instruction at the Marine Corps Schools at Quantico entitled 'Assault on a Fortified Position', based on Hunt's experiences on Peleliu. Here, Hunt's Company 'K', 3rd Bn, 1st Marines employed what became known as 'pin up' tactics, whereby a Marine team that consisted of a bazooka, two BARs, and an M-1 rifle would saturate a target with a voluminous amount of firepower. With the enemy troops pinned down inside their position, a Marine demolition team would move in 'for the kill'. One such team was armed with either a bangalore torpedo (a long iron pipe fitted at the end with an explosive, a detonating cap and fuse) or a satchel charge of dynamite, while another team would bring up two flamethrowers, protected by two riflemen who covered their approach to the target. Applied with deadly effect on Iwo Jima and especially at Okinawa, these tactics became known in time as the 'corkscrew and blow torch method' and were, as the overall commanding general of the Tenth Army and of the Okinawa assault, US Army General Simon Bolivar Buckner, commented later on: 'enough to destroy even the most steadfastly held Japanese defensive position'. As these Marine assault tactics demonstrated, even the most determined enemy or strongest defensive position, including the steel- and concrete-reinforced underground labyrinth of interconnecting defensive works created by the likes of a LtGen Tadamichi Kuribayashi, who was a master of defensive warfare, could be overcome with the right combination of firepower, manoeuvre, and determination.

The tactics adopted by Marine rifle regiments were born out of necessity, as the Japanese changed their own tactics from an offensive to a defensive system that had been designed to make the Marines and soldiers pay in blood for every inch of its island conquests. The Marines nonetheless designed suitable tactics that employed all of the arms that were organic to a Marine division. As the assault echelons fought their way across the islands and jungles of the South and Central Pacific areas, Marine tank–infantry teams, flamethrowers, and demolitions teams blasted and burned the determined enemy out of his elaborate system of defensive works, all of which culminated in a bloody war of attrition. Even though the amphibious assault from the strategic sense can be considered manoeuvre warfare, the fighting at ground level more closely resembled that of the attrition style of warfighting more common with battles fought during World War I. As Marine riflemen and demolition teams cleared the enemy from the ridges and valleys of these coral atolls, combat engineers cleared the land of deadly mines and booby traps. As Marine rifle companies set forth to clear out the entrenched enemy, tank–infantry teams provided flank security with 'Each cave position being attacked by fire until neutralized, then burned out with flamethrowers, and eventually sealed by demolitions.'

SUMMARY

As both the Marines and soldiers discovered, there were no easy victories in the Pacific War. Up against an adversary that chose death over surrender, the task of the ordinary Marine or soldier, artilleryman, tanker, or assault amphibian driver ('amtrac') became one of being able to deliver an overwhelming amount of firepower and destruction over a

battleground that changed from jungle to coral atoll, all within a matter of 15 months after the first landings on Guadalcanal in August 1942. Like the weapons Marines carried into battle in 1942, the basic tactics Marines went into battle with slowly evolved into the more sophisticated tank–infantry, or combined arms teams, that won not only

This Marine of the 2nd Marine Division, a survivor of the bloody battle for Tarawa, wears the typical uniform of a Marine at the end of 1943. As well as the camouflaged helmet cover, his uniform consists of a two-piece herringbone-twill suit, supplemented here by a captured water bottle and Japanese sword.

World War II but wars ever since. Many of these same tactics, in fact, had their origins in the desperate fighting that occurred during the last stages of World War I in 1918. The fighting in the South and Central Pacific likewise demonstrated that it was still an infantryman's war, and in the end it was the side that best employed its combined arms, in terrain that was oftentimes inhospitable and as demanding as the enemy they were up against, that emerged victorious.

Furthermore, the battlefield tactics and techniques employed by the Marines were ones that had evolved since World War I. The use of combined infantry, artillery and machine gun assaults gave way to the more sophisticated tank–infantry tactics employed with deadly effect on Saipan and Okinawa. As the Japanese adopted bunker and positional warfare, Marines devised even deadlier methods of extraction and destruction. As Marine riflemen and machine-gunners poured a voluminous amount of firepower into an enemy position, other leathernecks brought up bazookas, portable flamethrowers, and demolitions, and employed them with deadly effect. As the nature of the war shifted from one of defensive to offensive operations, so too did the training and organization of a Marine regiment. In fact, the tactical adjustments that the Marines caused the Japanese Army to make in its defensive-oriented strategy from 1943 onward necessitated a similar change in the methods of Marine training, tactical organization, and tables of equipment, that in time shaped and honed the combat skills of a Marine rifle regiment and created one of the best combined arms teams of the war. The training and battlefield techniques acquired by Marines in France during World War I, born out of necessity, and institutionalized

through the fire and carnage of the trenches, culminated with the momentous, often bloody, assaults in the Central Pacific during World War II. Marine training has always emphasized that only through 'fire and manoeuvre' can an enemy be defeated. In the preparation for its Pacific battles, the Marines honed those same battlefield techniques with deadly effect on the training grounds of Parris Island, San Diego, Quantico, and Camps Lejeune and Pendleton.

TOWARD A BATTLEFIELD EFFECTIVENESS

In the final analysis, the Marine who fought during World War II in the Pacific became a lethal killing machine, due largely to the impact of the Marine Corps' involvement in World War I, and its emphasis on individual basic infantry skills. In fact, it was during the interwar era that planners at HQMC disseminated many lessons of that war into an extremely lethal fighting doctrine employed by Marines during World War II in the Pacific. The tactics employed by the Marines came about largely through its commitment to

Below: A Marine assault and communications team go 'over the top' against a Japanese position. Radiomen were vital in coordinating attacks on the Japanese positions and support fire for the Marines on the ground.

Above: Sheer firepower was often the key to victory in defeating the Japanese. Here, a US Marine armed with a Thompson sub-machine gun and a BAR automatic rifleman provide supporting fire for a M4 Sherman in the attack.

hard training, discipline, courage, and a commitment to be the best – all this during a period of austere budgets and limited manpower. Marine officers such as MajGens George Barnett, John A. Lejeune, Wendell C. Neville, Ben H. Fuller, John H. Russell, and Eli K. Cole, as well as BrigGens Dion Williams and Robert H. Dunlap, and visionaries such as LtCol Earl H. Ellis and Richard M. Cutts saw in the Corps' advanced base mission a revolutionary new doctrine that, when coupled with the lessons learned during World War I by the individual Marine, ultimately ensured victory on the battlefields of the Pacific during World War II.

For all of the problems in recruiting and two major expeditionary missions in the 1920s, as well as the budgetary and manpower problems of the 1930s, Marine officers never lost sight of their commitment to training an excellent fighting machine. As the expeditionary years ended and Marines of all ranks returned to the classrooms and training depots, HQMC refocused its efforts toward the development of a viable and workable landing doctrine. Through the efforts of such leaders as Gens Thomas Holcomb, Holland M. Smith, Alexander

A. Vandegrift, and Charles Barrett, as well as countless field and company grade officers, the Marines implemented the landing doctrine that their predecessors had laboured with in the decade before World War II. While many of the latter did not live to see the fulfillment of their efforts, they nonetheless contributed to the outstanding victories of their successors in the jungles, on the coral atolls, and volcanic soil of the Pacific War. In a large sense, the success of the United States in World War II in the Pacific and in Europe can be largely attributed to those Marines and soldiers who clambered out of the trenches in 1918, as well as out of the whaleboats on Culebra and at Oahu in the 1920s. For it was their spirit that carried Marines and soldiers across the beaches of Guadalcanal, New Guinea, Tarawa, Saipan, Iwo Jima, Okinawa, North Africa, Sicily, Italy, and finally Normandy, to victory in 1945.

CHAPTER 5

Individual Weapons and Equipment of a Marine 1941–1945

> When fighting from island to island in their great drive across the Pacific towards the Japanese home islands, one factor that gave the Marines an advantage in their struggle was the sheer weight of their firepower. Every Japanese bunker or strongpoint was blasted until it was no more.

LIKE THE ORGANIZATION, training, and tactics used by the US Marine Corps during World War II, the weapons and equipment used also changed, as the tempo of the fighting intensified from island to island, and its nature changed from jungle warfare to the open warfare characteristic of the fighting from 1943 onward. This chapter will examine the weapons employed and uniforms worn by the individual Marine, as well as provide some background as to how and why HQMC adopted specific weapons and equipment. All the weapons and uniforms used by a front-line Marine were designed to withstand the climatic and geographic shifts in the fighting encountered in the Pacific Ocean area during World War II.

THE INDIVIDUAL ISSUE: HEADGEAR, PACKS AND WEBBING

Every Marine, regardless of his military occupational skill or MOS, had a standard issue of equipment that consisted of a field pack: a haversack; knapsack; belt suspenders; a cartridge belt, bayonet and scabbard (for those armed with the M1 Garand Rifle); a M1 Garand semi-automatic rifle, M1 Carbine, or a Browning Automatic Rifle (referred to as a

'BAR'); cleaning equipment that included a brush, oiler, an oiler and thong case, a leather sling for the rifle or BAR, and a web belt for the carbine; mess gear, which was a meat can with cover, knife, fork, and spoon; canteen with cup and cover; a first aid pouch; a poncho; a shelter-half with a pole, five pins, and a line known as a 'guy' line. Marines entering combat wore a steel helmet with a fibre lining and camouflage cover; gas mask; an entrenching tool, shovel, pick, mattock or machete.

Marine packs consisted of five different types. The Light Marching Pack consisted of only a haversack. The Marching Pack consisted of a haversack and belt suspenders, which carried rations, toilet articles, one undershirt, one pair of drawers, one pair of socks, mess gear, and poncho. The Field Marching Pack, used for field marches and training exercises, consisted of a haversack and a shelter-half or roll. The Transport Pack was worn while the Marine travelled by ship or rail, when blankets were not required. It consisted of a haversack and knapsack that carried additional clothing, such as an extra pair of shoes, trousers, shirt (jacket) undershirts, and drawers. The heaviest of the five was the Field Transport Pack, and was worn in the field and during route marches in the field. It consisted of the Transport Pack with a long blanket roll attached.

The Helmet

When the United States entered World War II, the helmet worn by the Marines was the old World War I-style M1917A1,

---

Left: A Marine flamethrower operator advances to provide covering fire against a Japanese position. Flame-throwers, first used by the Germans in World War I, were excellent weapons for neutralising fortified strongpoints.

similar to the British 'Brodie Pattern' helmet. In 1939, HQMC issued Marines an improved version of the M1917A1 helmet worn by the Marines during their occupation of Iceland in 1941–42. Padded in leather and painted with a rough olive drab paint, the helmet was worn until the summer of 1942, when the newer M1 Hadfield Manganese Steel Helmet, manufactured by the McCord Radiator Company of Detroit, Michigan, replaced them. The helmet, whose liner's suspenders were designed by the John T. Riddell Football Helmet Company, had been recommended by Brigadier General George S. Patton, Jr. It offered greater comfort to its wearer, and served throughout the US Armed Forces until its replacement in 1983 by the Kevlar 'Fritz' style helmet. Originally painted olive drab, Marines later used camouflaged covers over their helmets, which offered some cover and concealment during the jungle fighting on New Georgia and Bougainville, as well as when worn down over the back of the neck to protect against the sun at Tarawa.

In garrison Marines also wore a sun or pith helmet to protect them against the sun. Marines initially wore them during recruit training, though they found them to be both uncomfortable and constantly falling off. Nonetheless, the pith helmet remained in service during and after World War II in the field and at the recruit depots.

Marine Field Uniforms and Footwear

During the interwar period Marines did not have a 'field uniform' *per se*. Instead, for garrison work they normally wore a blue denim fatigue uniform, or a light khaki one for field duty in the tropics. In June 1940, HQMC replaced this uniform with a green cotton coverall uniform, which was worn until replaced on 10 November 1941 with a sage-green – although olive drab had been originally specified in the contract – herringbone twill cotton utility uniform. Herringbone twill was a popular material then used to manufacture civilian work clothing. The herringbone twill uniform, known as the 'utility uniform', consisted of a jacket (or blouse) and trousers. In 1943 a soft cap, made from the same herringbone material, and referred to as the 'chino', was produced to be worn as a garrison cover. The uniform had two large patched pockets sewn on the front skirts of the jacket, bronze-finished steel buttons each stamped with the words 'U.S. MARINE CORPS' in relief on them, while stenciled on the left breast pocket was a Marine Corps eagle, globe, and anchor in black

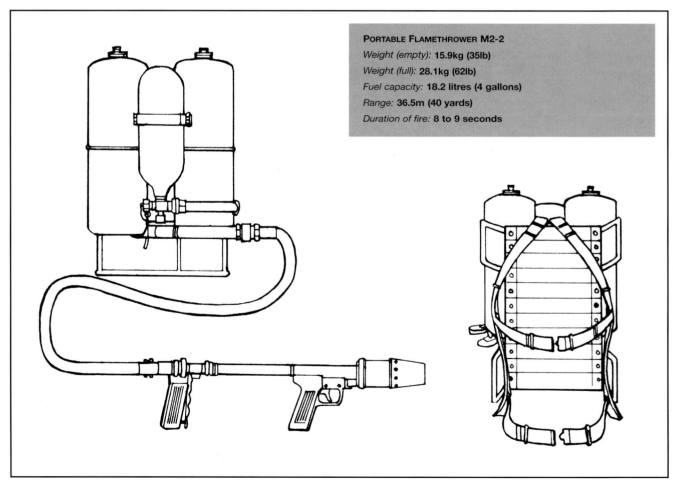

PORTABLE FLAMETHROWER M2-2

Weight (empty): **15.9kg (35lb)**

Weight (full): **28.1kg (62lb)**

Fuel capacity: **18.2 litres (4 gallons)**

Range: **36.5m (40 yards)**

Duration of fire: **8 to 9 seconds**

Above: A Marine poses in his Service Uniform Type 'C' at Marine Barracks, Quantico, VA in the mid-1930s. He is carrying an M1903 Springfield rifle, the standard firearm issue for the Marines until 1943, when it was replaced by the M1 Garand.

ink. The trousers, which had two slashed front and two rear patch pockets, were normally worn loose without the khaki leggings, and topped off by work shoes made from cord and rubber-soled rough-side out leather, known affectionately by Marines as 'boondockers'.

Prior to the landing on Tarawa in 1943, Marines adopted a camouflaged field uniform that did not become Corps-wide, however, and was primarily worn by Marine Raiders and Paramarines. For the most part, the standard field dress of a Marine was the herringbone utilities, camouflaged steel helmet, and 'boondockers', which proved to be an ideal uniform for the terrain of the Central Pacific and the later fighting on Iwo Jima and Okinawa.

Small Arms: Rifles, Pistols, and Automatic Rifles

During World War I and until 1943, the basic sidearm of a US Marine was the Model No 1903 Springfield .30in (7.62mm) bolt-action rifle. Marines demonstrated with deadly effect that a well-trained infantryman could accurately fire from 10 to 15 rounds per minute with great precision during World War I in the fighting at Belleau Wood. During the interwar

period, Marines continued to use the Springfield in such diverse places as Haiti, Dominican Republic, and Nicaragua. Marines, in fact, retained their venerable Springfields up to the campaign on Guadalcanal, when it slowly began to be replaced by the M1 Garand Rifle, a semi-automatic combat rifle that was both accurate and extremely durable – important factors when one considers the harsh climatic and geographic conditions of the South and Central Pacific. Along with the Springfields and Garands, Marines likewise carried into battle against the Japanese the famed Colt 1911A1 .45in (11.43mm) calibre pistol, Browning Automatic Rifle, Thompson submachine gun, and the M1 Carbine. All of these famed sidearms enabled Marines 'to close in with by fire and maneuver' against a determined Japanese opponent as they fought from island to island during World War II.

Following is a brief description of the weapons carried by Marines into battle during World War II.

1911A1 .45 Caliber Pistol

The automatic pistols, calibre .45 M1911 and M1911A1 are recoil-operated, magazine-fed, self-loading hand weapons. The pistol is a comparatively short-ranged weapon. Both the M1911 and M1911A1 are similar in operation, with only minor modifications to the latter insofar as its construction is concerned.

■ WEIGHT (WITH FULL MAGAZINE): 2.76 lbs (1.25kg); LENGTH: 8.59in (21.8cm); MAGAZINE CAPACITY: 7 rounds; LENGTH OF BARREL: 5.03in (12.78cm); MAXIMUM RANGE: 1600yd (1463m); MAXIMUM EFFECTIVE RANGE: 25yd (23m)

M1 Rifle .30 Caliber 'Garand'

The M1 Garand Caliber .30 rifle was the standard firearm of US Marines during World War II from 1943. Half of a Marine rifle company were equipped with M1s. It is a gas-operated, clip-fed, air-cooled, semi-automatic shoulder weapon. Its principal characteristic is its rapid mechanical operation, which enabled the individual Marine to deliver a large volume of accurate fire upon any designated point or area within range. The effective range of the M1 rifle is 600 yards. It was without a doubt one of the best combat rifles ever manufactured.

■ WEIGHT: 9.5lb (4.3kg); LENGTH (WITHOUT BAYONET): 43.6in (110cm); LENGTH OF BARREL: 24in (61cm); AVERAGED RATE OF AIMED FIRE PER MINUTE: 30 rounds; CLIP CAPACITY: 8 rounds; MAXIMUM RANGE: 3500–3550yd (3200–3246m)

M1903 .30/.30 Caliber 'Springfield'

The Model 1903 .30 Caliber 'Springfield' breech-loaded, magazine-fed, bolt-operated, shoulder-fired weapon had been in continuous Marine Corps field service since 1903, and remained in its inventory through the Korean War as its sniper rifle. The M1 Garand replaced it as the primary weapon used by Marine rifle companies in early 1943. The average number of shots a Marine could achieve with this rifle was 10 rounds per minute.

■ WEIGHT: 8.9lb (4kg); LENGTH (WITHOUT BAYONET): 43.2in (109.7cm); LENGTH (WITH BAYONET): 55.2in (140cm); LENGTH OF M1 BAYONET: 12in (30.5cm); WEIGHT OF BAYONET: 1lb (.45kg); MAGAZINE CAPACITY: 5 rounds; MAXIMUM RANGE: 2850yd (2606m) ; MAXIMUM EFFECTIVE RANGE: 600yd (584m)

M1 Carbine, .30 Caliber Rifle

The M1 Carbine was a .30 (7.62mm) calibre, shortened version of a rifle first carried by the US Cavalry. Half of the total personnel in a Marine regiment carried the carbine, primarily officers and noncommissioned officers. Like the M1 Garand, the carbine is a gas-operated, semi-automatic, air-cooled, self-loading shoulder-fired weapon. Marine officers often carried the Carbine instead of the .45in (11.43mm) calibre pistol.

■ WEIGHT (WITH FULL MAGAZINE AND SLING): 5.75lb (2.6kg); LENGTH: 33.5in (85cm); MAGAZINE CAPACITY: 15 rounds; MAXIMUM RANGE: 2200yd (2011m); MAXIMUM EFFECTIVE RANGE: 300yd (274m)

Browning Automatic Rifle ('BAR')

The Browning Automatic Rifle, more commonly referred to as 'BAR', Caliber .30 M1918A2, is a .30in (7.62mm) air-cooled, gas-operated, magazine-fed shoulder weapon and was carried by the designated automatic rifleman in each fire team. It can fire in either the automatic or a semi-automatic mode. Despite its weight of over 20lb (9kg), it is a very mobile weapon that can deliver a cyclical rate of 350 to 550 rounds per minute in the automatic mode, or 120–150 rounds per minute in short bursts of three to five rounds.

■ WEIGHT: 20lb (9kg); LENGTH (OVERALL): 47.8in (121.4cm); MAGAZINE CAPACITY: 20 rounds; CYCLICAL (NORMAL) RATE OF FIRE: 550 rpm; CYCLICAL (SLOW) RATE OF FIRE: 350 rpm; MAXIMUM RANGE: 5500yd (5029m); MAXIMUM EFFECTIVE RANGE: 600yd (548m)

Thompson Submachine Gun Model 1928

The Thompson submachine gun was first introduced into the Marine Corps' arsenal during the interwar era, and was used by Marines in Nicaragua and China. It can deliver a rapid rate of fire of .45in (11.43mm) calibre ammunition, and can be fired in automatic or semi-automatic mode. It is an air-cooled, recoil-operated, magazine-fed shoulder-fired

weapon. During the fighting in Nicaragua, it was found to be extremely effective in close-in fighting. During World War II, NCOs and primarily Marine Raiders and Paramarines carried it instead of the Reising submachine gun. It could use either a straight box magazine or a drum that contained 50 rounds.

■ WEIGHT: 9lb, 13oz (4.45kg); LENGTH: 33in (83.8cm); MAGAZINE (BOX) WEIGHT: 2lb (0.9kg); MAGAZINE (DRUM) WEIGHT: 2lb (0.9kg); MAGAZINE CAPACITY (BOX): 20 rounds; MAGAZINE CAPACITY (DRUM): 50 rounds; MAXIMUM RANGE: 1700 yd (1554m); MAXIMUM EFFECTIVE RANGE: 350yd (320m)

Rcising Submachine Gun Type 55

The Reising submachine gun had been designed and developed by noted gun inventor Eugene Reising. The original patent for the Reising was 1940, and in the intervening period as the US military prepared for war in 1941, the Reising submachine gun filled an important gap in small arms ordnance. There were two different models made, the Type 50 and Type 55. The Type 50 had a wood stock and a Cutts compensator on the muzzle, which prevented it from 'jumping' up after being fired. The Type 55 had a folding metal shoulder stock which swivelled on the wooden pistol grip. This version of the Reising had been intended for tank crewmen, parachutists, and Raiders who required a compact weapon. It

Below: A Marine officer poses with his M1 Carbine and camouflage poncho. As the war progressed, items of camouflage crept into Marine uniforms. The ponchos were rainproof, and could be used to erect a basic shelter.

Above: Here, a group of Marines from the 6th Marines pose in their winter field gear, along with fur caps, in Iceland. Marines were sent to Iceland when British troops previously stationed there were withdrawn for use in the fighting in North Africa.

fired the same .45in (11.43mm) calibre ammunition used in the Thompson submachine gun. There were a total of 100,000 Reising submachine guns produced between 1940 and 1942. Most were used by the Marines during the Guadalcanal campaign. The Type 55 was used extensively by the Paramarines and the Raiders. Due to its propensity to jam the Reising was withdrawn from frontline service in favour of the M3 'Grease Gun' and the BAR. Nonetheless, the Reising, when used under more favorable conditions, was preferred by leathernecks for its lightness and accuracy, as opposed to the more unreliable Thompson submachine gun.

■ WEIGHT: 6lb (2.72kg); LENGTH (STOCK EXTENDED): 31.25in (79.4cm); LENGTH (STOCK RETRACTED): 22.5in (57cm); CALIBRE: .45in (11.43mm); CYCLICAL RATE OF FIRE: 450–550rpm; MAGAZINE CAPACITY: 20 rounds

SUPPORT WEAPONS

Supporting Marines in the field were light and heavy machine guns, mortars, 'bazookas', flamethrowers, rifle and hand grenades, and other pyrotechnics. When employed effectively, they proved a deadly combination that enabled Marines to advance 'by fire and maneuver' against determined enemy strongpoints in the South and Central Pacific areas. Much of the doctrine used in the employment of machine guns and mortars stemmed from the Corps' experience during World War I in France, and in fighting the Sandinista guerrillas in Nicaragua (1927–1933). According to Marine General Lemuel

C.Shepherd, who commanded the 6th Marine Division during the campaign on Okinawa, Marines in fact experimented with several methods in order to improve the effect of mortar fire, and thereby increase the firepower of a regimental mortar battery. Colonel Samuel Harrington, commanding officer of the 2nd Bn, 5th Marines suggested the idea of 'firing mortars in batteries', much like the 75mm (2.95in) pack howitzers. As Shepherd later commented, 'In other words, get them [the 81mm (3.2in) mortars] lined in on a certain stake so that you could fire several major salvos of mortars just as though you were firing a battery of artillery.' There is some evidence that Marines used this method in several instances, particularly on Peleliu and later on Okinawa.

Support Weapons Inventory

M1919A4 Browning Light Machine Gun .30 Caliber
Each Marine rifle company had a light machine gun platoon that consisted of one officer and 36 enlisted men armed with 12 machine guns: 6 Browning M1919A4 .30in (7.62mm) calibre light machine guns and 6 Browning M1917A1 .30in calibre heavy machine guns. Marines normally employed these weapons in a static defensive role, as well as in support of offensives by Marine infantry.

Above: A Marine machine gun team carries a Browning .30in (7.62mm) calibre water-cooled machine gun and ammunition on Bougainville in 1943. Note the hose for the cooling mechanism wrapped around the machine gun's barrel.

Normally, when used in the offensive role, Marines used six machine guns according to the type of terrain and situation while the remaining six guns were held in reserve. It could also be used in the anti-aircraft role.

■ WEIGHT: 31lb (14kg); WEIGHT OF GUN (WITH PINTLE AND TRAVERSING MECHANISM): 35.75lb (16.2kg); WEIGHT OF GUN AND TRIPOD: 49.75lb (22.6kg); LENGTH (OVERALL): 41.11in (104.4cm); MAXIMUM USABLE RATE OF FIRE PER MINUTE: 150 rounds; CYCLICAL RATE OF FIRE: 450–550 rounds per minute; CAPACITY OF M1 AMMUNITION BOX: 300 rounds

Browning .30 Caliber M1917A1 (HMG)

The M1917A1 Heavy Machine Gun is a recoil-operated, belt-fed, and water-cooled weapon similar to the M1919A4 Light Machine Gun. The specifications are exactly the same, other than the fact the HMG has a water plug assembly where a hose runs to a water container in order to keep the barrel from overheating, and thus preventing the machine gun from jamming when fired.

M2 Caliber .50 Machine Gun (Heavy)

The M2 .50in (12.7mm) calibre machine gun was perhaps the deadliest heavy machine gun in the US Marine arsenal.

Marines used it in an offensive and defensive role. The weapon was likewise used in an anti-personnel, anti-aircraft, and anti-vehicle role.

■ WEIGHT (M3 TRIPOD, T&E PINTLE): 128lb (58kg); LENGTH: 65in (165cm); CREW: 2; MAXIMUM RANGE: 7941yd (6850m); MAXIMUM EFFECTIVE RANGE: 2034yd (1860m); RATES OF SUSTAINED FIRE: 75rpm; RATES OF RAPID FIRE: 75rpm; RATES OF CYCLIC FIRE: 400–500rpm

Mortars

M19/M2 60mm Mortar

The 60mm (2.36in) mortar was perhaps the most powerful company weapon available to Marine commanders. It was a Marine commander's personal light and portable fire support weapon, and has been referred to as 'a weapon of opportunity'. A 60mm mortar is always under the control of a company commander, and thus is always available for 'on call' fire. The mortar section includes one officer, (a first or second lieutenant) and 19 enlisted Marines. The section had a headquarters of one officer and two enlisted men. During World War II there were three mortar sections, with each squad consisting of a corporal, who was the squad leader, and five privates first class or privates. Each section had three mortars, and could be supplemented by other 60mm mortars or 81mm (3.2in) mortars found on the battalion level.

■ WEIGHT (M19 MORTAR, BASEPLATE AND M5 BIPOD): 47.75lb (21.65kg); WEIGHT (M2 MORTAR WITH BASEPLATE AND M5 BIPOD): 42lb (19kg); RANGE (HIGH EXPLOSIVE SHELL): 2000yd (1828m); RANGE (WHITE PHOSPHOROUS): 1650yd (1508m); RANGE (ILLUMINATING SHELL): 1150yd (1050m); RATE OF FIRE, MAXIMUM: 30–35rpm; RATE OF FIRE, SUSTAINED: 18–20rpm

81mm Mortar

The 81mm (3.2in) mortar could be found on the regimental level, and is a smoothbore, muzzle loading, high angle of fire weapon. The mortar barrel is a single unit, while the mount consists of two units, the bipod and the base plate. The M3 Baseplate is circular, and is approximately 21in (53.5cm) in diameter, and of one-piece construction.

■ WEIGHT (M3 BASEPLATE, BIPOD, AND BARREL): 87.5lb (39.6kg); OVERALL LENGTH: 51in (129.5cm); MAXIMUM RANGE: 4000yd (3657m); MAXIMUM RATE OF FIRE: 12 for two minutes; SUSTAINED RATE OF FIRE: 3 for two minutes

M18 Rocket Launcher or 'Bazooka'

The launcher or 'bazooka' is a simple open tube-type shoulder weapon. It can fire either high explosives or other types of rockets from standing, kneeling, sitting, or prone positions. It has a smooth bore, is electrically operated, and is loaded at the breech. Its primary function was as an anti-tank weapon, though Marines used it to reduce fixed enemy positions such as pillboxes, caves, and fortified bunkers. The Marine Corps assigned them to assault platoons for an attack against enemy mechanized units and strong points.

■ LENGTH: 61in (155cm); WEIGHT: 10.3lb (4.67kg); POINT TARGET RANGE: 25 to 300yd (23–274m); AREA TARGET RANGE: 300 to 650yd (274–594m); CREW: 2

M2-2 Flamethrower (portable)

The M2-2 Flamethrower entered service in early 1942, though Marines had used flamethrowers during the interwar era, after German assault groups first employed flame weapons during World War I. It was carried by one Marine who was armed with a .45in (11.43mm) calibre pistol as a sidearm. It had two main parts, the Tank Group and the Gun Group. The M2-2 Flamethrower could get through the ports and slits of pillboxes, bunkers, and other fortifications with flame and smoke. It could set fire to shelters, and had the ability to shoot around corners or at blind angles. During World War II, when the Japanese dug or hid themselves in caves, the flamethrower proved to be an excellent weapon in mopping-up operations. It likewise proved to be an excellent jungle and urban weapon in the Solomons, and in fighting in built up areas on Saipan, Tinian, and Okinawa. There was one drawback to the flamethrower, however, and that was the danger it held if the person carrying it accidentally compressed the trigger, which often resulted in their being incinerated.

■ WEIGHT (EMPTY): 35lb (15.9kg); WEIGHT (TANK GROUP – FULL): 62lb (28.1kg); WEIGHT (GUN GROUP): 8lb (3.6kg); WEIGHT (GUN AND TANK GROUPS): 70lb (31.7kg)

Rifle Grenades

There were several types of rifle grenades employed by the Marines during World War II. Fired from the M1 Garand Rifle with the assistance of an attached adapter, the fuze of the grenade was armed after the grenade and adapter left the launcher, which could throw grenades about 175 yd (160m).

High Explosive Fragmentation Grenades

M9A1 Anti-tank Grenade

Fragmentation Hand Grenade MK IIA1

M17 Impact Fragmentation Rifle Grenade

Both the M9A1 anti-tank rifle grenade and Mk II fragmentation hand grenade had a bursting radius of 10yd (9.1m), and could penetrate nearly all Japanese armoured fighting vehicles.

Smoke Grenades

M19 Smoke White Phosphorus (WP) Rifle Grenade

M20 Smoke Rifle Grenade (HC)

M22 Colored Smoke Rifle Grenade

M23 Smoke Streamer Rifle Grenade

Pyrotechnic signals were equipped with a fin assembly so that they could be fired from launchers, and came in clusters or parachutes in white, green, amber, and red.

Hand Grenades

The Marines used five types of grenades in World War II:

Fragmentation: contained an explosive charge in a body that shattered into fragments when it burst.

Offensive: contained a high-explosive charge in a paper body, designed for concussion effect.

Chemical: contained a chemical agent that produced a poisonous or irritating effect on the body. Chemical grenades could also furnish a screening or signal smoke, an incendiary or burning action or any combination of these.

Practice: contained a reduced charge and looked and acted something like fragmentation grenades.

Training: contained no explosives or chemicals; used for familiarity purposes.

BROWNING M2 HB

Calibre: **12.7mm (0.5in)**

Weight: **38.1kg (84lb)**

Cyclic rate of fire: **450-575rpm**

Muzzle velocity: **884mps (2900ftps)**

Feed: **110-round metal-link belt**

CHAPTER 6

Marine Support Weapons 1941–1945

Although their amphibious role required that the Marines Corps' equipment should be easily transportable, the Marines could nonetheless command an impressive array of support equipment to help them in their task. Vehicles like the LVT or 'Amtrac' were vital to the Marines' success.

BESIDES A VAST ARRAY of individual weapons Marines had at their disposal during the island battles of World War II, they could likewise call on the support of Marine Corps aircraft as well as such weapons as tanks, assault amphibian vehicles, anti-tank weapons, artillery and anti-aircraft guns, as well as explosives and demolitions, and truck-mounted rocket launchers. By the time of the Okinawa campaign in April 1945, Marines could expect nothing but the best in support weapons at all tactical and operational levels, as they set out to assault the strongly defended inner ring of the Japanese home islands.

ARMOURED FIGHTING VEHICLES (TANKS AND 'AMTRACS')

M3A1 Stuart Light Tank

A late production of the original M3 light tank, the M3A1 had a crew of 4 (commander, loader, gunner, driver), a gyro-stabilized M5 37mm (1.45in) gun and carried two .30in (7.62mm) calibre machine guns on either side of the sponsons on the left and right side, as well as one attached to the cupola. It had a maximum speed of 36mph (58km/h), and could travel across country at 20mph (38.2km/h) (much slower in

Left: A M1 1-ton Cargo truck mounted with 4.5in (114.3mm) rockets. Marines who operated these units were called 'Buck Rogers' men after the famous cartoon strip of the day. They could saturate an area with one salvo.

swamps). It could ford up to 3ft (90cm) of water, and had a radius of 70 miles (112.6km). It carried 116 rounds of 37mm (1.45in) ammunition, and 6400–8720 .30in (7.62mm) calibre rounds.

M4A2 Sherman

The most widely used American tank of World War II was first used by the Marines on Tarawa in November 1943. The M4A2 carried the standard 76mm (3in) gun and had one .50in (12.7mm) calibre and one internally-mounted .30in (7.62mm) calibre machine gun. It could travel at 24–29mph (38.6–46.6km/h) on roads and cross country could travel between 15–20mph (24.1–32.1km/h). It had a crew of 5 (commander, gunner, loader, driver, co-driver), and could ford 3ft (90cm) of water.

M7 'Priest' 105mm Self-Propelled Gun

The M7 'Priest' could be used as either an anti-tank or anti-personnel weapon, or as a 'bunker buster'. It carried a 105mm (4.1in) howitzer, and could also carry up to 13 Marines internally up to the front lines. Marines used the M7 'Priest' extensively on Okinawa. Armament was a single 105mm (4.1in) howitzer with a .50in (12.7mm) calibre machine gun, and it carried 69 rounds of 105mm (4.1in) ammunition internally. It could ford up to 4ft (121.9cm) of water, and had a road speed of 25–26mph (40.2–41.8km/h). Cross-country speed of the M7 was up to 15mph (24.1km/h). It had a crew of 7 that included commander, driver, and 5 gun crewmen.

Above: Marines ride into battle aboard heavily-armored LVTs in late 1944. The amphibious LVT gave the Marines an added dimension in their landing operations, and they would have found it difficult to progress as fast as they did across the Pacific without them.

M3 M1A1 Halftrack with 75mm gun (T-12 GMC)

The Marines converted several standard vehicles to increase the fire support offered to Marine infantrymen. One of the vehicles so converted was the M3 Halftrack that carried either the 75mm (2.95in) pack howitzer or the standard 105mm (4.1in) howitzer. Marines used these extensively throughout the island-hopping campaigns in the Pacific during World War II. With a crew of 5 (driver, co-driver, commander, and two gun crewmen) Marines used the M3A1 extensively throughout the Pacific War as an anti-tank, infantry-support weapon.

Landing Vehicle Tracked LVTs I–V

The original LVT, or 'Amtrac', was designed by inventor Donald Roebling, and entered US Marine Corps service in mid-1940. First used to ferry supplies across the beach, the LVT saw front-line combat service during the assault on Tarawa. While the LVT itself was not armed, subsequent versions were upgraded with armoured sheets welded to their sides for added protection.

LVT(A)-1

Landing Vehicle Tracked (Armored) Mk I, had a crew of 6, carried one 37mm (1.45in) gun; two .30in (7.62mm) calibre machine guns, and one .50in (12.7mm) calibre machine gun. It could travel at 25mph (40.1km/h) on land and 6mph

(9.6km/h) on water, and carried 104 rounds of 37mm ammunition. Later in the war, Marines replaced the 37mm gun with an E7 flamethrower that proved extremely effective in the fighting for Bougainville and New Georgia.

LVT(A)-2

The LVT(A)-2 had the same characteristics as the LVT(A)-1, with the exception that the LVT(A)-2 had no armament and was used exclusively as a troop carrier. It was used primarily by the US Army.

LVT-3 'Bushmaster'

Developed by the Borg Warner Corporation, the LVT-3 entered service during the Okinawa campaign (April 1945). It had a far superior hydraulic automatic transmission that enhanced its tactical mobility afloat and ashore.

LVT(A)-4

The LVT(A)-4 had the same characteristics as the LVT(A)-1 with the exception that the LVT(A)-4 had a turret armed with a 75mm (2.95in) howitzer, and carried one .50in (12.7mm) calibre machine gun. It was the most extensively used and most successful of the LVT family of vehicles. Later in 1943 the LVT(A)-4 had the Canadian-built 'Ronson' flamethrower attached in place of the 75mm gun. Marines also experimented with mounting rocket launchers on its sides.

LVT(A)-5

The LVT(A)-5 had the same characteristics of the LVT(A)-4 but had a gyro-stabilized gun and power-traversed turret. It did not enter field service until after World War II.

ARTILLERY

During World War II, the US Marine Corps used several basic types of field artillery, ranging from the 37mm (1.45in) anti-tank gun to the 155mm (6.1in) 'Long Tom', used by Marine Defense Battalions. The 'workhorse' of the Marine Corps during the entire war was the 75mm (2.95in) 'pack' howitzer, a portable, easily-transportable field piece that entered service in 1931, and saw limited combat duty in Nicaragua (1931–33) prior to the withdrawal of the Marines in January 1933. As the fighting shifted from jungle warfare to 'bunker-busting' in the Central Pacific and on Iwo Jima and Okinawa, the 105mm (4.1in) howitzer replaced the venerable 75mm due to its increased velocity and ability to destroy the increasingly hardened Japanese bunkers and fixed defensive positions. Marines likewise employed 20mm (.79in), 37mm (1.45in), and 90mm (3.5in) anti-aircraft guns as base and airfield defence weapons. In fact, during World War II, the Marines used a number of light anti-aircraft artillery and heavy machine guns in both the weapons groups of the defense battalions and, later on, immediately ashore with the landing force during an amphibious assault. Marine officers employed them many times in a dual role against ground and air targets. Organized into batteries, they eventually came to make up an important part of the Marine combined arms teams.

Towed Artillery

M3A1 37mm Anti-tank Gun

Developed by the US Army in the 1930s, and used as a replacement for the French 37mm (1.45in) Puteaux gun, the M3A1 was adopted by the Marines due to its excellent penetrating ability, its mobility, and accuracy. While the weapon was used by both the Army and the Marines, the Marines used it against the thin-skinned Japanese tanks and as an anti-personnel weapon when armed with canister. It had a crew of 4, and was transported on a 4x4 quarter-ton truck. It had a maximum range of 500yd (457m).

M1A1 75mm Pack Howitzer

The first prototype of the M1A1 75mm (2.95in) Pack Howitzer emerged in 1920, entering field service with the US Army in 1927. It first entered Marine service in 1931. The M1A1 used during World War II entered service in 1934. During the war it served as an excellent infantry support and anti-tank weapon. Re-equipped with pneumatic tyres and towed by jeeps and halftracks, the 75mm was redesignated the M8. It had a crew of 5; and fired HEAT, Smoke, High Explosive; it could fire a short burst rate of 6rpm; and a sustained rate of 3rpm. The gun's maximum range was 10,000yd (10,396m).

M101 105mm Howitzer

Designed as a replacement for the French-built 75mm howitzers used by the Marines, the 105mm (4.1in) first entered service in 1934 and was designated the M2 105mm howitzer. The final version of the 105mm was the T5, that had a higher rate of fire, and was easily transportable. Crew: 8; towed by a 2-ton truck; weight 4475lb (2030kg); maximum range 12,325yd (11,270m); rate of fire (maximum)10rpm; sustained rate of fire 3rpm.

M1A1 155 mm Howitzer

The 155mm (6.1in) howitzer replaced the M1917 French Schneider 155mm used by the US Marine Corps between 1920 and 1941, and was standardized in 1941. Marine defense battalions used the M1918 'GPF' 155mm gun and later the M1A1 as a ground artillery weapon. It was towed either by a 5-ton truck or M4 tractor. Crew: 15. Weight: 30,600lb (13,879kg). It had great mobility and became the standard heavy artillery weapon in the later stages of the war.

4.5in Rocket Launcher Detachment

The 4.5in Rocket Launcher teams were armed with three 4.5in (114.3mm) rocket launchers, each mounted on a 4 x 4 1-ton truck that carried 12 rockets. Each team could fire 36 rounds within a matter of seconds, 'blanketing' an area. First formed into units by the Marines in 1943, they were used during the fighting on Bougainville and on New Britain at Cape Gloucester. They proved extremely effective during the fighting on Saipan in 1944, and later on Iwo Jima and Okinawa. In fact, on Iwo Jima, 4.5in rocket launcher crews (known by Marines as 'Buck Rogers' teams after the legendary cartoon strip of the time) fired an estimated 30,000 shells.

Towed Anti-Aircraft Guns

M3 3in Anti-Aircraft Gun

Adopted for Marine Corps defense battalion use as an anti-aircraft gun in 1939, the M3 fired a 12.87lb (5.85kg) shell and had a maximum horizontal range of 14,780yd (13,514m) with a 10,000yd (9144m) ceiling. It had an eight-man crew, and could fire 25 rounds per minute.

M1A1 90mm Anti-Aircraft Gun

The M1A1 became the standard anti-aircraft gun in the US Marine Corps in 1941. It fired a 23.4lb (10.6kg) projectile, at

Left: A Marine 155mm (6.1in) howitzer prepares to fire on a Japanese position. Although naval guns were often available to give fire support, the Marines made extensive use of their own artillery resources.

a distance of 18,890yd (17,273m) and had a vertical range of 11,273yd (10,308m). It had a 10-man crew who could fire 28 rounds per minute. The Marine Corps' 90mm (3.54in) anti-aircraft guns generally came ashore early on during an amphibious landing in order to provide immediate AA defence on the beachhead. It had a dual role in that it could be directed against ground targets as well.

M1 40mm Automatic Anti-Aircraft Guns

Both the 37mm (1.45in) and 40mm (1.57in) Bofors automatic anti-aircraft guns were used by the Marines against low flying enemy aircraft. The M1 40mm Bofors became the standard anti-aircraft gun after 1942. It was recoil operated, and could fire 120 rounds per minute with a range of over 4 miles (6.4km). The 40mm could be quickly brought into action by a good crew and, according to Marine Corps statistics, was directly responsible for 50 percent of all Japanese airplanes shot down between 1944 and 1945.

Oerlikon 20mm Anti-Aircraft Gun

Known as the 'twin-twenty' because it was mounted on a wheeled carriage, Marines could quickly bring the 20mm (.78in) Oerlikon into action, and fired explosive, armour-piercing and incendiary shells at a rate of 450 per minute at a maximum range of 4800yd (4389m). Mobile, reliable, and accurate, as well as being able to fire a high volume of ammunition, the 20mm Oerlikon accounted for 32 percent of identified aircraft shot down by Marine anti-aircraft gunners between 1942 and 1944.

M2 Browning .30 water-cooled Anti-Aircraft Machine Gun

The M1917 Browning water-cooled machine gun, when mounted on a M2 anti-aircraft mount, proved to be an effective anti-aircraft weapon, and was used to defend artillery and anti-aircraft positions, as well as beach and ground defences, with a two-man crew. Personnel for the M2 came from the defense battalions.

MINES

During World War II, The US Marine Corps employed four types of anti-tank mine, the M1A1, M5, M6, and light M7 mines, as well as the M2A3 anti-personnel mine.

M1A1 Anti-tank Mine

The M1A1 anti-tank mine, the standard US mine used in the war. It weighed 11lb (4.98kg), with 6lb (2.7kg) of TNT encased in a metal shell. A pressure of 500lb (226.8kg) or more could detonate the mine on its fuze or 250lb (113.4kg) on its top edge (spider).

Above: A Marine anti-aircraft 20mm (.78in) Oerlikon team on Guadalcanal stands ready to repel a Japanese air attack on Henderson Airfield in October 1943. The Oerlikon was a very effective short-range anti-aircraft weapon.

M5 Anti-tank Mine

The M5 was perhaps the most deadly mine used, due to its shell being made of undetectable ceramic. It contained 5.6lb (2.5kg) of explosives encased in a ceramic bowl, and could be set off by 275–425lb (124.7–192.8kg) of pressure.

M6 Anti-tank Heavy Mine

The M6 was an answer to the heavier German tanks developed during World War II. It weighed 20lb (9kg), of which 12lb (5.4kg) was explosives. A weight of 300–600lb (136–272kg) could set off the mine. What made the M6 extremely deadly were the attached anti-lifting devices, which prevented an enemy from safely removing it from the ground.

M7 Anti-tank Light Mine

The M7 light anti-tank mine was developed for use in minefields laid hastily to provide perimeter security. It could be lifted and refitted into the ground as necessary. It weighed about 4lb (1.8kg), contained 3lb (1.36kg) of explosive, and could be set off by 150–250lb (68–113kg) of pressure.

M2A3 Anti-personnel Mine

The M2A3 anti-personnel mine was far more deadly than a 60mm (2.36in) mortar, as it could send projectiles about 6ft (1.8m) into the air, and produced more casualties. Its fuze was ignited by either a pull or pressure fuze, with pressure from either 3–6lb (1.36–2.7kg) (pull fuze), or pressure from 20lb (9kg) once the pressure cap was depressed by the object or person.

US MARINE INSIGNIA

CAP BADGE

Dress Uniform: Officers

Dress Uniform: O.R.s

Service Uniform: Officers

Service Uniform: O.R.s

SHOULDER

Lieutenant General

Major General

Brigadier General

Colonel

Lieutenant Colonel

Major

Captain

1st Lieutenant

SHOULDER

2nd Lieutenant

Chief Warrant Officer

Warrant Officer (Marine Gunner)

ARM

Sergeant Major Master Gunnery & 1st Sergeants

Master, Tech, Q.M., & P.M. Sergeants

Gunner Sergeant

ARM

Tech. Drum-Major & Supply Sergeants

Platoon Sergeant

Staff Sergeant

Sergeant

Corporal (Summer Service Dress)

Private 1st Class (Dress Uniform)

BIBLIOGRAPHY

Government Documents

Adjutant and Inspector's Office, *Correspondence of the United States Marine Corps*, Record Group 127, National Archives, Washington, D.C.

Annual Reports of the Major General Commandant of the US Marine Corps to the Secretary of the Navy for the years 1919–1939. (Washington, D.C., Government Printing Office, 1920–1940).

Field Service Regulations: U.S. Army, 1923. (Washington, D.C., Government Printing Office, 1924).

'How the Guam Operation was Conducted' 'Japanese Ground Self Defense Forces', Published respectively in the October–December 1962 in the journal *Kambu Gakko Kiji*, 24 June 1963.

Primary Sources

Farrington, A. C. *The Leatherneck Boys: A PFC at the Battle for Guadalcanal.* (Manhattan, KS, Sunflower Press, 1995).

Lejeune, J. A. *Reminiscences of A Marine.* (Philadelphia/Quantico, Dorrance and Company and The Marine Corps Association, 1930/1979).

Smith, H. M. and Finch, P. *Coral and Brass.* (Washington, D.C., Zenger Publishing, Co., 1947).

Vandegrift, A. A. *Once A Marine: The Memoirs of General A. A. Vandegrift, Commandant of the Marine Corps.* (Quantico, Va., Marine Corps Association, 1982).

Secondary Sources

Guidebook For Marines. (Washington, D.C., Leatherneck Association, 1948).

Alexander, J. H. *The Marine Assault on Tarawa.* (Washington, D.C., HQMC, 1993).

_____. *Closing In: Marines in the Seizure of Iwo Jima.* (Washington, D.C., History & Museums Division, HQMC, 1994).

_____. *The Final Campaign: Marines in the Victory on Okinawa.* (Washington, D.C., HQMC, 1996).

_____. *Storm Landings: Epic Amphibious Assault Battles in the Central Pacific.* (Annapolis, MD: Naval Institute Press, 1997).

_____. *A Fellowship of Valor: The Battle History of the United States Marines.* New York: HarperCollins, 1997).

Appleman, R. E., Burns, J. M., Gugeler, R. A., and Stevens, J. *United States Army in WWII: The War in the Pacific: Okinawa* (Washington, D.C., Dept of the Army, 1948).

Averill, G. P. *Mustang: A Combat Marine.* (Novato, Presidio Press, 1987).

Ballendorf, D. A., and Bartlett, M. L. *Pete Ellis: An Amphibious Warfare Prophet. 1880–1923.* (Annapolis, MD., Naval Institute Press, 1997).

Bartlett, M. L. *Lejeune: A Marine's Life, 1867–1942.* Columbia, S.C. USC Press, 1991).

Bergerud, E. *Touched With Fire: The Land War in the South Pacific.* (New York: Penguin Press, 1996).

Brown, L. A. *The Marine's Handbook.* (Annapolis, MD: Naval Institute Press, 1939).

Buckner, D. N. *A Brief History of the 10th Marines.* (Washington, D.C., History & Museums Division, 1981).

Champie, E. A. *Brief History of the Marine Corps Base and Recruit Depot: San Diego, California.* (Washington, D.C., Historical Branch, G-3, HQMC, 1962).

_____. *A Brief History of Marine Corps Recruit Depot, Parris Island, South Carolina.* (Washington, D.C., Historical Branch, G-3, HQMC, 1962).

Chapin, J. C. *Top of the Ladder: Marine Operations in the Southern Solomons.* (Washington, D.C., HQMC, 1997).

_____ *And A Few Marines: Marines in the Liberation of the Philippines.* (Washington, D.C., HQMC, 1997).

_____. *Breaking the Outer Ring: Marine Landings in the Marshall Islands.* (Washington, D.C., HQMC, 1994).

_____. *Breaching the Marianas: The Battle For Saipan.* (Washington, D.C., HQMC, 1994).

Clifford, K. J. *Progress and Purpose: A Developmental History of the U.S. Marine Corps.* (Washington, D.C., History and Museums Division, 1973).

Condit, K. W., Diamond, G., and Turnbladh, E. T. *Marine Corps Ground Training in World War II.* (Washington, D.C., Historical Branch, G-3, HQMC, 1956).

Condit, K. W., Johnstone, J. H., and Nargele, E. W. *A Brief History of Headquarters Marine Corps Staff Organization.* (Washington, D.C., Historical Division, HQMC, 1970).

Condit, K. W., and Turnbladh, E. T. *Hold High the Torch: A History of the 4th Marines.* (Nashville, Ten: The Battery Press, 1989).

Cressman, R. J. *A Magnificent Fight: Marines in the Battle for Wake Island.* (Washington, D.C., HQMC, 1992).

_____ and J. M. Wenger. *Infamous Day: Marines At Pearl Harbor, 7 December 1941.* (Washington, D.C., HQMC, 1992)

Donovan, J. A. *Outpost in the North Atlantic: Marines in the Defense of Iceland.* (Washington, D.C., HQMC, 1992).

Frank, B. M. and Shaw, H. I., *Victory and Occupation, History of U.S. Marine Corps Operations in WWII. Volume V.* (Washington, D.C., Historical Branch, G-3, HQMC, 1968).

Garand, G. W., and Strobridge, T. R. *Western Pacific Operations: History of U.S. Marine Corps Operations in WWII. Volume IV.* (Washington, D.C., Historical Division, G-3, HQMC, 1971).

Gayle, G. D. *Bloody Beaches: The Marines at Peleliu.* (Washington, D.C., History & Museums Division, HQMC, 1996).

Harwood, R. *A Close Encounter: The Marine Landing on Tinian.* (Washington, D.C., History & Museums Division, HQMC, 1994).

Heinl, R. D., Jr., and Crown, J. A. *The Marshalls: Increasing The Tempo.* (Knoxville, TN., Battery Press, 1991).

Hoffman, C. W. *Saipan: The Beginning of the End.* (Knoxville, TN., Battery Press, 1988).

Hoffman, J. T. *From Makin to Bougainville: Marine Raiders in the Pacific War.* (Washington, D.C., HQMC, 1995).

_____. *Silk Chutes and Hard Fighting: U.S. Marine Corps Parachute Units in WWII.* (Washington, D.C., HQMC, 1999).

_____. *Once A Legend : 'Red Mike' Edson of the Raiders.* (Novato: Presidio Press, 1994).

Hough, F. O. *The Island War: The United States Marine Corps in the Pacific.* (Philadelphia: J. B. Lippincott, Co., 1947).

_____. *The Assault on Peleliu.* (Knoxville, TN, Battery Press, 1990).

Hough, F. O., Ludwig, V. E., and Shaw, H. I. *Pearl Harbor to Guadal-canal. History of U.S. Marine Corps Operations in WWII. Volume I* (Washington, D.C., Historical Branch, G-3, HQMC, 1958).

Jones, W. D., Jr. *Gyrene: The World War II United States Marine.* (Shippensburg, Pa., White Maine Publishing Co., 1998).

Jones, W. K. *A Brief History of the 6th Marines.* (Washington, D.C., History & Museums Division, HQMC, 1987).

Krulak, V. H., *First To Fight. An Insider's View of the U.S. Marine Corps.* (Annapolis, MD., Naval Institute Press, 1984).

Lorelli, J. A. *To Foreign Shores: U.S. Amphibious Operations in World War II.* (Annapolis, MD, Naval Institute Press, 1995).

Mackin, E. E. *Suddenly We Didn't Want to Die: Memoir of A World War I Marine.* (Novato, Ca., Presidio Press, 1993).

Melson, C. D. *Condition Red: Marine Defense Battalions in World War II.* (Washington, D.C., HQMC, 1994).

_____. *Up the Slot: Marines in the Central Solomons.* (Washington, D.C., History & Museums Division, HQMC, 1993).

Metcalf, C. H. *A History of the United States Marine Corps.* (New York: G. P. Putnam's Sons, 1939).

Miller, J. M. *From Shanghai to Corregidor. Marines in the Defense of the Philippines.* (Washington, D.C., HQMC, 1997).

Millett, A. R. *Semper Fidelis: The History of the United States Marine Corps.* (New York: Macmillan Publishing, Co., 1991).

_____. *In Many A Strife: General Gerald C. Thomas and the U.S. Marine Corps, 1917–1956.* (Annapolis, MD.: Naval Institute Press, 1993).

Musicant, I. *The Banana Wars. A History of United States Military Intervention in Latin America From the Spanish-American War to the Invasion of Panama.* (New York: Macmillan Publishing, Co., 1990).

Nalty, B. C. *Cape Gloucester: The Green Inferno.* (Washington, D.C., History & Museums Division, HQMC, 1994).

_____. *The Right to Fight: African-American Marines in World War II.* (Washington, D.C., HQMC, 1995).

O'Brien, C. J. *Marines in World War II. Liberation: Marines in the Recapture of Guam.* (Washington, D.C., HQMC, 1994).

Reeder, R. P. et al. *Fighting on Guadalcanal.* (reprinted Quantico, Va. Marine Corps University, FMRP-12-110, MCCDC, Quantico, Va., 1991).

Rentz, J. N. *Bougainville and the Northern Solomons.* (Washington, D.C., Historical Section, Division of Public Information, HQMC, 1948).

Santelli, J. S. *A Brief History of the 7th Marines.* (Washington, D.C., History & Museums Division, HQMC, 1980).

_____. *A Brief History of the 4th Marines.* (Washington, D.C., Historical Division, G-3, HQMC, 1970).

Shaw, H. I. *Opening Moves: Marines Gear Up For War.* (Washington, D.C., History & Museums Division, HQMC, 1991).

Shaw, H. I., Nalty, B. C., and Turnbladh. *Central Pacific Drive. History of U.S. Marine Operations in WWII. Volume III.* (Washington, D.C., G-3, Historical Branch, HQMC, 1966).

Shaw, H. I., and Kane, D. T. *Isolation of Rabaul. History of U.S. Marine Corps Operations in WWII. Volume II.* (Washington, D.C., G-3, Historical Branch, HQMC, 1963).

Shaw, H. I. *First Offensive: The Marine Campaign For Guadalcanal.* (Washington, D.C., HQMC, 1992).

Sledge, E. B. *With the Old Breed At Peleliu and Okinawa.* (New York: Oxford University Press, 1981).

Smith, C. R. *Securing the Surrender: Marines in the Occupation of Japan.* (Washington, D.C., HQMC, 1997).

Spector, R. H. *Eagle Against the Sun: The American War Against Japan.* (New York: The Free Press, 1985).

Stockman, J. R. *The Battle for Tarawa.* (Washington, D.C., Historical Section, G-3, HQMC, 1947).

Thompson, P. W., Doud, H., and Scofield, J. *How the Japanese Army Fights.* (reprinted, FMRP-12-22, U.S. Marine Corps, MCCDC, Quantico, Va., April 1989).

Updegraph, C. L., Jr. *U.S. Marine Corps Special Units of World War II.* (Washington, D.C., History & Museums Division, HQMC, 1977).

Wright, D. *A Hell of A Way to Die: Tarawa: 20-23 November 1943.* (London: Windrow & Greene, Ltd., 1996).

INDEX